Cambridge Elements ≡

Elements in Historical Theory and Practice
edited by
Daniel Woolf
Queen's University, Ontario

HISTORIOGRAPHIC
REASONING

Aviezer Tucker
University of Ostrava

CAMBRIDGE
UNIVERSITY PRESS

Shaftesbury Road, Cambridge CB2 8EA, United Kingdom

One Liberty Plaza, 20th Floor, New York, NY 10006, USA

477 Williamstown Road, Port Melbourne, VIC 3207, Australia

314–321, 3rd Floor, Plot 3, Splendor Forum, Jasola District Centre,
New Delhi – 110025, India

103 Penang Road, #05–06/07, Visioncrest Commercial, Singapore 238467

Cambridge University Press is part of Cambridge University Press & Assessment,
a department of the University of Cambridge.

We share the University's mission to contribute to society through the pursuit of
education, learning and research at the highest international levels of excellence.

www.cambridge.org
Information on this title: www.cambridge.org/9781009565226

DOI: 10.1017/9781009324489

First published 2024

A catalogue record for this publication is available from the British Library

ISBN 978-1-009-56522-6 Hardback
ISBN 978-1-009-32450-2 Paperback
ISSN 2634-8616 (online)
ISSN 2634-8608 (print)

Historiographic Reasoning

Elements in Historical Theory and Practice

DOI: 10.1017/9781009324489
First published online: December 2024

Aviezer Tucker
University of Ostrava

Author for correspondence: Aviezer Tucker, avitucker@yahoo.com

Abstract: *Historiographic reasoning* from evidentiary inputs is sui generis. Historiography is neither empirical, nor self-knowledge, nor a genre of fiction or ideology. Historiographic reasoning is irreducible to general scientific or social science reasoning. This Element applies Bayesian insights to explicate historiographic reasoning as probable. It distinguishes epistemic transmission of knowledge from evidence from the generation of detailed historiographic knowledge from multiple coherent and independent evidentiary inputs in three modular stages. A history of historiographic reasoning since the late eighteenth century demonstrates that there was a historiographic scientific revolution across the historical sciences in the late eighteenth and early nineteenth centuries. The underdetermination of historiography by the evidence, counterfactual historiographic reasoning, and false reasoning and other fallacies are further explained and discussed in terms of the probabilistic relations between the evidence and historiography.

Keywords: historiography, history, evidence, reasoning, the historical sciences

ISBNs: 9781009565226 (HB), 9781009324502 (PB), 9781009324489 (OC)
ISSNs: 2634-8616 (online), 2634-8608 (print)

Contents

1 Historiographic Reason: An Introduction

What right do historians have to tell everybody else what happened, did not happen, and may have happened in history? They have reasons. Reasoning is the inference of probable conclusions from premises. *Historiographic* reasoning is a type of inference whose conclusions refer to past states of affairs, to history, and whose premises are present evidential inputs that preserve information transmitted by past events, from history. Historiographic reason recognizes and decodes evidential information to infer what happened in history. This Element argues that historiographic reasoning is sui generis: Historians reason from evidence to historiography by utilizing forms of reasoning unique to the historical sciences.

This project may face the objection that it does not matter for historiography, the disciplinary practices of historians, and the results of their research, because historiographic reasoning is *tacit*. Historiographic institutional practices may display the hallmarks of what Collins (2010) called "collective tacit knowledge." Training transmits tacit knowledge through apprenticeships that cannot be formalized or articulated, for example in a textbook. Tacit knowledge must be acquired directly, through social embedding, by being in the company of people who possess it, such as senior historians and fellow apprentices. People who possess tacit knowledge display informed behavior without being aware of it. They find the articulation of their tacit knowledge challenging, but it does not matter for their success in deploying tacit knowledge to reliably infer knowledge of history. Conversely, theoreticians who can articulate explicitly the contents of implicit knowledge are not necessarily able to produce it. An accomplished dolphin does not need to know hydrodynamics any more than a hydrodynamics engineer needs to know how to swim. Great authors need not have an explicit knowledge of syntax and grammar, and expert grammarians are not necessarily great authors. Lennon and McCartney reputedly could not read or write musical notes, and many music teachers who are accomplished in music theory and notation cannot compose. One may anxiously believe about historiography that "if it works, don't analyze it!" If the sausages are tasty, it may not be a good idea to inspect how they are made because it may destroy the appetite.

But what if the prestige historians enjoy and their own professional self-respect are founded on avoiding methodological questions about reasoning and rationalizing tacit practices? Historians, who possess only tacit knowledge, cannot exclude this frighteningly disturbing possibility because they do not know what they are doing self-reflectively. This anxiety may partially account for the absence of seminars in historiographic epistemology and methodology in high-status academic history departments that dominate the limited market for producing academic historians, where knowledge of historiographic reasoning is expected to be acquired tacitly through practice, absorbed by osmosis as it were. It may be advisable for aspiring "dolphin calves" to skip studying hydrodynamics to join a prestigious pod and learn tacitly from their elders how to swim.

Yet, hydrodynamics, philology, and musicology have justified *raisons d'être*. The old joke about two psychotherapists running into each other by coincidence and exclaiming spontaneously: "You are fine; how am I?" reflects a deep truth: People and professionals often have a clearer and less biased view of others than of themselves. Understanding the implicit norms of reasoning of historiography should benefit from a theoretically explicit approach. Though it is unnecessary to know the rules of grammar or musical theory to author stylized literature and compose popular music, it surely helps.

Reason, including historiographic reason, is always threatened by the passions. As La Bruyere (quoted in Elster 1999, 337) put it: "Nothing is easier for passion than to overcome reason, but the greatest triumph is to conquer a man's own interest." Passions affect the *beliefs* of their adherents. When passion overcomes reason, beliefs become narrative representations of passions rather than probable conclusions of reliable processes of reasoning from evidence. For example, hate or fear can cause beliefs that the objects of hate or fear must have committed horrible crimes. When historiographic narratives represent passions, evidence cannot convince or dissuade the passions. Choosing between alternative or conflicting historiographic narratives is then undertaken not on the rational basis of evidence and reasoning, but on the basis of "authenticity," the strength of the passions that the narrative represents (Tucker & Garfinkle 2018). Historiographic reasoning stumbles and falls then on its head: Instead of reasoning from the evidence to a historiographic conclusion, it moves backward from passionately "authentic" historiography to evidential or factual claims that reflect rather than justify the narrative representation of the passions. This process of the decline and fall of reason and its replacement with passions has happened previously, for example when the irrational passions of Treitschke trumped the historiographic reasoning and rationality of Ranke. Totalitarian movements of the left and right subjected historiographic reasoning to their political passions. Authoritarian governments fitted state-sponsored historiographic narratives to their political passions and interests, to manipulate, disorient, and above all control the historical consciousness of their subjects, to "engineer their souls" and ignore the evidence or even destroy it. Orwell captured in his *1984* the nature of totalitarian historiography in his portrayal of the "Ministry of Truth" that is in charge of deleting historiographic evidence according to the shifting desired ideological conclusion; changes in the ideologically desired historiography determine the evidence, rather than the other way round.

When historiographic reason and reasoning are under attack and threatened by political passions, reliance on tacit knowledge and the implicit institutional normative traditions of the historiographic community may prove too feeble to fortify and hold the rational dam against the pressure of the much stronger passionate flood. Tacit norms can be revised equally tacitly, unnoticed, because they are amorphous. Explicit and formal analysis of historiographic reasoning is more difficult to revise unnoticed. An explicit and formal analysis of historiographic reasoning is likely to resist the onslaught of the passions more effectively than tacit knowledge, in a new age of strong political and other tribal passions, magnified through the echo chambers of social media.

Another challenge to this project may come from the claim that there is no historiographic *reasoning*, because knowledge of history is not inferred from premises, either because historians "observe" history directly, or because historiography is a type of self-knowledge, or because historiography is an expression of historical consciousness. Alternatively, it may also be argued that there is no *historiographic* reasoning because the reasoning that historians employ is indistinct from types of reasoning scientists or social scientists use. Finally, if historiography is an ideologically constructed fiction that has neither premises nor conclusions, there is no *historiographic reasoning*. I start this Element then by arguing against denials of historiographic reasoning and for the sui generis nature of historiographic reasoning.

If there is sui generis historiographic reasoning, it should be analyzed explicitly. Bayesian probabilistic models are particularly appropriate and useful for this task because they formalize the conditional relation between evidence and epistemic outputs such as knowledge and degrees of belief – credences. Bayesian models can explain historiographic reasoning as inferences from historiographic evidence of probable knowledge of history, the past. They can further account for and explain historiographic change, how and why historiographic reasoning revises previously held historiographic beliefs in light of new evidence. In a broader context, we live in a digital information age in which many of the advances in fields of knowledge as disparate as computer science predictive modeling of language, geological inferences of probable locations of underground deposits of natural resources, and inferences of phylogenic ancestries are founded on probabilistic and Bayesian models. Historiography has been ahead of this curve because historians had been information scientists who employed, albeit informally, Bayesian models for the inference of the origins of information-preserving evidence before formal information science was invented and even slightly before Laplace introduced formal Bayesian models for inferences from testimonies at the close of the eighteenth century.

Evidence may *transmit* or *generate* knowledge. When historical evidence transmits knowledge, the premises of historiographic reasoning, the evidence, transmit more or less reliable information to historiographic conclusions. The conclusions then cannot be more reliable than their premises. For example, when the evidence is the testimony of an eyewitness, historians judge its reliability as sufficient or insufficient to transmit knowledge, to retransmit information from reliable evidence to their readers while discarding unreliable evidence. By contrast, historiographic reasoning *generates* knowledge when the evidential premises are not reliable enough to transmit knowledge, but their historiographic conclusions pass the epistemic threshold for knowledge. For example, when there are several eyewitness testimonies that are individually insufficiently reliable to be believed, if they cohere and the coherence is unlikely to be random or the product of transmission of information between the witnesses or the information channels that transmitted the information to them, they may generate together conclusions that are sufficiently probable to constitute knowledge of history. Generative historiographic reasoning is then analyzed as proceeding in three stages that infer successively that the evidentiary inputs preserve coherent information from *some* historical common origin of the information; the information transmission channels that connected the common origin with the units of the evidence; and properties of that common origin – the historical event or process which, put together, compose historiography.

Historiographic reasoning has a history. Historiographic reason can achieve self-consciousness by tracing this history. In the second half of the eighteenth century, historiography underwent a scientific revolution when historiographic reasoning began to *generate* knowledge of history as well as transmit it. This historical-scientific revolution spread from philology to the other historical sciences over a century. This section traces the origins of this historiographic scientific revolution.

Historiographic reasoning is limited by its premises, by the cruel entropic censorship of the evidence – loss of useful information in transmission and mixture with noise, and by available information theories that can decode information in evidence. When the premises are insufficient to determine a historiographic conclusion, the output of reasoning may be a probability distribution over a range of possibilities. The analysis of underdetermined historiography is therefore part of the analysis of historiographic reason.

Historiographic reasoning infers what happened, may have happened, and could not have happened in history. Yet, it is also possible to reason about what did not happen but could have happened differently in history, about historiographic counterfactuals. It is debatable whether there is counterfactual historiographic reasoning, and if so, how it relates to "factual" historiographic reasoning. Arguably, the two forms of reasoning partly overlap.

Epistemic contextualism argues that the criteria for knowledge are not absolute. Equally probable conclusions of reasoning may be probable enough to be considered knowledge in some contexts, but insufficiently probable in other contexts. Section 13 explores epistemic contextualism in historiography.

Reasoning is invalid when conclusions do not follow from premises, and false when the premises are not true. The previous analysis of valid historiographic reasoning sets a standard useful for the identification of types of invalid historiographic reasoning that draw improbable conclusions about history from true premises, and of false reasoning that are founded on false premises.

Finally, I compare historiographic reasoning about human history to reasoning in other historical sciences to conclude that they belong to the same epistemic "family," distinguishable from other sciences by their sui generis form of reasoning.

2 "Empiricist" Historiography without Reasoning

If historiography is empirical, historiographic knowledge is composed of descriptions of observations of concrete particular historical events. Empirical historiography would not require reasoning because it would be describing direct observations. Meinecke (1972, LV), for example, characterized "historicism" as "the substitution of a process of individualizing observation for a generalizing view of human forces in history."

However, *history*, by definition, happened in the past. Therefore, it cannot be perceived through the senses, and *historiography*, research that draws inferences about history – the past, cannot be an observational science. The historical train had always left the station before historians could arrive. Therefore, everything knowable about history requires evidence and historiographic reasoning. Accordingly, historiography cannot be an empirical science of human nature modeled after Newtonian physics, though some historians borrowed rhetorical elements of empiricism to legitimize their enterprise, especially during the formation of the discipline in the intellectually empiricist nineteenth century.

Collingwood (1956), Murphey (1973, 1994, 2009), and Goldstein (1976, 1996) noted the obvious: Historiography cannot observe historical events; it uses evidence and reasoning to justify inferences of information about historical events. There are no given historical facts: Historiography "is a science whose business is to study events not accessible to our observation, and to study these events inferentially, arguing to them from something else which is accessible to our observation, and which the historian calls 'evidence' for the events in which he is interested" (Collingwood 1956, 251–252). The immediate, primary, subject matter of historiography is evidence, not observations.

The logical-empiricist philosophical school stipulated that knowledge is comprised exclusively of observation sentences that describe accurately and comprehensively facts in the world and their a priori logical relations. If so, since the past cannot be observed, there can be no knowledge of history and no historiographic reasoning. Michael Dummett (1978) initially concluded that sentences about the past are not *assertoric*, they are neither true nor false, because they have no observational truth conditions. Later, though, Dummett (2004) himself, in lectures he gave at Columbia University (that I attended) came to reject this skeptical conclusion as "repugnant." He developed instead a "justificationist" view that bases historiographic assertions on *subjunctives*: What an observer in the past *would have* observed. For example, if a natural historian asserts that a meteor killed the dinosaurs, it means that *had there been* an observer then, the observer *would have observed* a meteor hit Earth, and then the darkening of the sky from the debris, the death of much of the vegetation, and eventually the death of the dinosaurs at the top of the food chain.

Subjunctive justificationism may resolve the semantic problem that concerned Dummett: How can historiographic sentences assert without direct observational justification? But epistemically, justificationism eliminates a small problem by creating a bigger one, because it is more difficult to infer from the evidence what a historical observer *would or would not have observed* had they been present during a historical event than to simply justify propositions about what happened, because the first requires more evidence than the second. Epistemically, if there is sufficient evidence to reason what happened, reasoning about subjunctive observations is redundant at best, and overly restrictive at worst, because there may be sufficient evidence for inferring what happened but insufficient evidence for inferring what an observer *would have* observed. For example, historical linguistics can infer much about the proto–Indo-European language, but not enough to infer what a contemporary observer would have heard proto–Indo-Europeans speaking. Some of the events and processes historians infer would not have been observable even by contemporaries because they were slow and gradual processes, or the events occurred in unobservable minds. Nobody could have observed the Industrial Revolution or the Renaissance. Contemporary observers could have observed respectively machines and migrations from fields to factories, and classically inspired anthropocentric art. Ideational mental changes could not have been observed directly. As Roth (2012, 322) noted, most of what historiography refers to, including the objects of Danto's (1985) narrative sentences that refer to two distinct times (e.g. "the assassination of Archduke Ferdinand in 1914 started the First World War"), were not and could not have been observable by contemporaries, since nobody in Sarajevo in 1914 could have observed "the First World War."

Murphey (2009, 16–17) chided Dummett for ignoring that actual, rather than subjunctive, historical observations by contemporaries are *testimonies*. The evaluation of testimonies requires reasoning and evidence for their reliability. Testimonies cannot be the self-evident factual observations that the logical positivists dreamt would be the foundations of meaning and truth.

Dummett (2004) nevertheless formulated elegantly the asymmetry between past and future: "[W]e assign to the past those events capable of having a causal influence upon events near us, so that we can receive information from them and of them, but have no means of affecting them; and we assign to the future those events that we can affect, but from which we can receive no information" (86). Dummett should have drawn an obvious conclusion from this fine formulation: What can be known about the past is reasoned from the information it transmitted to its future, the evidence.

3 Historiography as Self-Knowledge without Reason

Another form of knowledge that is immediate and therefore does not require reasoning is self-knowledge. Self-knowledge is founded on the epistemically privileged and unmediated access of consciousness to the self. For example, you know right now how exciting this Element appears to you and whether your little toe is itchy, because you have immediate unmediated and privileged access to yourself that others are not privy to. If the relation of historiography to history is of a conscious subject to itself, no process of reasoning is required. Historiography may then *express* rather than *represent* history, since representation stands in for something distinct from itself whose knowledge requires reasoning (D'Amico 1989).

If historiography expresses historical introspection, the historical entities that introspect and express must exist continuously from the historical past to the historiographic present, and possess an intuitive faculty for inner perception over time. If historiography is an expression of introspection, historiographic disagreements do not result from different premises or reasoning, but express different authentic identities, or at least inauthentic self-deceptions. Debates between historiographic expressions of introspection can be over who occupies the privileged position of self-knowledge to express a historical identity, who does not, and who inauthentically denies their epistemic privileges to express self-deception or even self-hatred if they are critical of the identity they express. Reason and evidence cannot resolve disputes over who has authentic historical identity. The debates within political philosophy over the meaning of authentic positive liberty (see Dimova-Cookson 2019) demonstrate that such disputes are inevitable, yet cannot be resolved even when the authenticity in question is universally human and hence accessible in principle to all those who debate it. Utopian schemes about historiography as a "polyphony" of expressions of different identities and traditions that combine together into a harmony (Serrier & Michonneau 2019) sound nice but are likely to result in cacophonies of strident siren calls that express conflicting identities that cannot possibly be combined into a consistent, let alone harmonious, historiographic narrative. Such historiographic inconsistencies cannot be resolved by deliberative negotiations, because it is impossible to negotiate on identity and self-consciousness, and it is impossible to appeal to the higher court of the evidence. Further, if historiography is the expression of identitarian self-consciousness and traditions, each constructed identity inhabits its own monad-like bubble historical universe that cannot be punctured by competing identities. The result would be historiographic fragmentation when each identity sings its own songs that cannot harmonize into a choir or a historiographic oratorio. Without common reasoning and evidence, there are no grounds for deliberation about history between different identities that inhabit distinct epistemic bubbles, any more than different faiths could negotiate their liturgies to harmonize them into a single ecumenic prayer accepted by all faiths. Each group's historiography becomes unmoored from the ground of evidence and reason to set sail on the winds of intuitions or self-delusion hither and thither.

The fragmentation of a common perception of the world and the loss of grounds for communication are problems that have recently become associated with the results of social media echo chambers (see Ressa 2023), but not with historiography. This social-epistemic difference between historiography and social media, the fact that historians do not live in epistemic bubbles and echo chambers but communicate on the common grounds of evidence and reasoning, is one indicator that historiography is founded on reasoning and evidence rather than expressions of identities and their intuitive introspections.

The introspective interpretation of historiography has evolved in conjunction with historical processes of *construction* of new historical identities. To borrow Ernest Gellner's (1983) *bon mot*, nationalists (and other cross-sectional identitarians) consider historical identities "sleeping beauties" that had existed in a dormant state before the expressive "kiss" of the historian awakened them into self-consciousness. Nineteenth-century European nationalist historians, like the

Czech František Palacky, constructed new national identities by authoring national historiographies, on the nonexclusive epistemic foundation of national expressive introspection. Nationalist historiographies had to be expressed exclusively by introspective nationalists and could not be written by "others," who could not have had privileged access to the nations' histories.

Writing after the denouement of European nationalism in the Second World War, Gadamer (1989) abstracted national identities to construct *traditions* as the fundamental ontological entities that unite the historical hermeneutic subject and object to maintain historiography as an expression of self-knowledge. Since then, intellectuals have volunteered to "awaken" a plethora of other "sleeping beauty" identities in addition to national identities by claiming to express their historical self-knowledge. Some of these identities are bureaucratically constructed and come with budgetary incentives for identity self-expressing historians. The epistemology of these identity-based representations holds that historiography is not or should not reason from the evidence, but rather represent self-consciousness, to conclude that only fish can have the required self-consciousness to be marine biologists.

The self-consciousness of constructed identities such as nations is at best metaphorical. At worst, it assumes obscurantist spooky collectivist ontology founded on necrophiliac phantasies about mind-melding with the ancestors. But had historiography been founded on self-consciousness, the social structure of historiography would have been of independent, at most weakly interacting, identity bubbles, such as those of nineteenth-century nationalist cultures that included constructed historiographies along with national literatures in the vernacular and national music and opera.

Self-knowledge can also be universalist, of humanity rather than of particular tribal identities. Idealist philosophers of history, who did not consider themselves to be expressing a particular historical identity, like Vico and Hegel, still attempted to found knowledge of the past on self-consciousness, by constructing universal ontologies such as Vico's (1984) *modifications of the human mind* and Hegel's *spirit*. However, idealist philosophies of history disagreed about the contents of that universal historical self-consciousness and expressed it inconsistently. Worse, there is no method to adjudicate between conflicting expressions of self-consciousness, whether universalist or particularist-identitarian, since they do not *reason* from publically accessible evidence, but from their private introspections of constructed historical entities whose existence is doubtful. There are no independent public grounds for preferring one idealist philosophy of history over another and since they are inconsistent, they cannot all be true at the same time.

The intellectual relations between historians may be modeled sociologically as interconnected nets rather than as political, identity, or idealist bubbles. Historians group themselves professionally according to types of evidence by political history, economic history, cultural history, and so on, or types of reasoning associated with the information theories of schools like the Cambridge school of intellectual history or the Annales school. Historians debate their methodologies and the reliability of their evidence, but usually do not condemn each other's identities or degrees of authenticity as identity artists do. A broad consensus among historians of extremely diverse and conflicting identities is unlikely if historiography is the expression of the immediate unreasoned intuitive self-knowledge of collective identities.

4 Irrational Historiography: Fiction and Ideology

If historiography is pure art, fiction, myth, or ideology, it has no knowledge to offer and it is a category mistake to associate it with reasoning. Artists, authors of literary fiction, and ideologists do not reason and their outputs are not subjected to tests of truth or validity. Art is subjected to aesthetic judgments. Ideology is judged by its usefulness for mass mobilization for the achievement of political goals. Hayden White (1987, 1992) defended the view that much of historiography is ideological fiction, and different stories about the past should be judged according to aesthetic or ideological criteria: "[H]istorical narratives ... are verbal fictions, the contents of which are as much invented as found and the forms of which have more in connection with their counterparts in literature than they have with those in the sciences" (1978, 82).

This rejection of historiographic reason is at odds with the history and social structure of historiography. There are artistic and ideological social "bubbles" of likeminded people who share aesthetic or political values. Members of these groups, say, Impressionists and Abstract Expressionists, or monarchists and anarchists, disagree but do not reason to convince each other; if they try they usually fail – people change artistic or ideological identities as a result of "conversions" that are often deeply emotional rather than rational. Reason does not change artistic styles and ideologies. By contrast, most historians agree on most of their historiographic outputs, and even more so on their epistemic inputs, the evidence. This creates a space for debates about reasoning from evidential inputs to historiographic outputs. This degree of consensus resembles the history and social structure of science more than of art or ideology.

Broad consensus that distinguishes a community of experts from a socially comparable "control group" can have three and only three explanations (see

Tucker 2014): shared biases of the experts, random agreement, or shared specialized knowledge. For example, in an opinion survey that asks: "Do you believe that massive public investment in historiographic research and education will greatly improve civic virtue?" Undoubtedly, virtually all historians would reply affirmatively. This consensus would far exceed the average agreement on this issue in a control group of non-historians. But the best explanation of this consensus would be professional bias – any profession would tend to agree that massive transfer payment to its members is beneficial to society. Taxpayers who would have to foot the bill for this largesse may be less enthusiastic, however. Other agreements can be random. If a group of historians goes for dinner and each member of the group spontaneously orders the same item from the menu, this agreement may reflect neither bias nor expertise. One historian may like the dish, another may consider it the healthiest, yet another may have read a recommendation, and yet another was instructed by his doctor to order that meal (for example, in 1989 I attended the Collingwood centenary conference at Oxford University's Pembroke College. When we organized for dinner, the senior philosopher Nathan Rotenstreich excused himself, explaining that he was a diabetic and at the advice of his doctor had to eat a particular dish at a particular restaurant. Rotenstreich took out of his jacket a note from his doctor, and read to us: "I should eat only at the restaurant, McDonald's . . . "). Fashions are initially based on random agreement that is later enforced by social pressure. Some academic fields indeed follow fashions without reasons. Finally, historians may agree because they share access to the same public evidence and they agree on the reasoning from that evidence, whereas nonexperts do not know the evidence or the shared reasoning processes that the experts utilize.

If historians reach consensus because of biases, they must either have identical biases; or different biases should somehow, miraculously, converge to generate the same historiography. Historians have different institutional affiliations, nonprofessional interests, passions, political loyalties, and so on, so apart from joint professional interest in the wealth, power, and prestige of historians, they have no apparent common biases that can plausibly correlate with the historiography they agree on, more than comparable control groups of nonhistorians. The historiographic consensus is too broad and consistent to plausibly follow random agreement, and it has lasted too long to be a passing fad. Academic fashions happen; but they never last more than a generation and retire along with the cohort that was pressured to follow the fashion to be employable. When a new generation seeks to replace their elders, they tend to do so in the name of a new fashion. For example, in literary theory, Marxism gave way to structuralism, then post-structuralism, then postmodernism that is already in the process of being replaced with as yet something else. Reasoning from primary sources by contrast has never gone out of fashion for a couple of centuries now because it was not adopted to conform to a fashion but because it is conducive for historiographic discovery. By elimination then, specialized knowledge based on special though publicly available evidence and reasoning explains best the broad and long historiographic consensus, and the gap between expert historiographic knowledge and lay opinions.

Still, Hayden White (1987) would retort that rationality, reason, is itself a type of ideological bias: "For subordinant, emergent, or resisting social groups, this recommendation – that they view history with the kind of 'objectivity,' 'modesty,' 'realism,' and 'social responsibility,' that has characterized historical studies since their establishment as a professional discipline – can only appear as another aspect of the ideology that they are indentured to oppose." (81) Historiographic reasoning is reduced then to a social structure, "centers of established political power and social authority" are contrasted with the alternative bias of "subordinant, emergent, or resisting social groups." This Manichean scheme adapts the philosophy of historiography to life in the Marvel Universe, so pleasantly familiar to American undergraduates. It shares the groundless oligarchic myth perpetuated by Plato and Aristotle that considers the lower classes and slaves irrational and hence incapable of personal or social self-governance, while holding the elite to be the paragon of reason, irrespective of the numerous follies and passionate irrational blunders of ancient (and modern) social elites. Hayden White and other members of the "Feu-cult" made irrationality respectable, if not great, again (Tucker 2024). Enlightenment philosophers, by contrast, used reason rather than irrationality to undermine irrational social hierarchies

The reduction of historiographic reason to an ideology can acknowledge that the historiographic community that reasons from evidence is heterogeneous in many respects. Yet, arguably it is homogenous at least in sharing *cognitive values*. Cognitive values determine which statements are worthy of being considered knowledge. Since shared cognitive values are necessary for forming beliefs, the historiographic expertise hypothesis may have to be qualified as relative to a particular bias, a shared set of cognitive values. Expertise then is just an intermediate variable between shared cognitive values and correlated beliefs. Yet, consensus on cognitive values, just like the consensus on their historiography, can result from bias, random coincidence, or expertise. The emergence of historiography as a science was accompanied by a shift from traditional cognitive values that valued faith, ancient wisdom, and above all tradition as justifications of beliefs about the past, to critical values that valued evidence and its critical examination followed by reasoning. These new values were adopted because historians believed they were more conducive to the discovery of knowledge of history. The "conduciveness to knowledge" explanation of the consensus on cognitive values can be tested by comparing it with bias and random coincidence hypotheses. If historiographic agreement on cognitive values results from shared biases, cognitive values would have to correlate with some social or cultural biasing factors. But it is quite difficult to explain the appeal of these cognitive values to very different experts in comparison with socially similar control groups of non-experts. The conduciveness of these cognitive values to knowledge seems like the best explanation for why experts adopted them (Tucker 2014). Since critical cognitive values have dominated historiography since the later eighteenth century, they cannot be explained away as fashionable fads.

To use Windelband's (2015) distinction between *origins* of ideas the historical context of their emergence, development, and reception, and *validities,* what make the outcomes of origins acceptable or not, historiographic reasoning validates historiography irrespective of its origins. The existence of origins does not have to bias the validation process. For example, Marxism is among the main origins of the subdiscipline of economic history because it drew attention to the historical significance of economic structures and change. However, the validity of economic historiography has nothing to do with this origin. Javier Solana advised politicians that "history is history, leave it to the historians." He did not advise historians to leave politics to the politicians, but perhaps he should have.

Other philosophies of historiography deny historiographic reasoning by combining "empiricism" with aestheticism. Ankersmit (1995, 2001, 2012) divided historiography between descriptive "empirical" propositions about individual historical facts, and narratives that, like artistic styles, are about themselves as much as about their objects, history. Artistic representations may describe an object like the Houses of Parliament in London (by Turner, Monet, Derain, or Bansky) or the Grand Canal in Venice (by Canaletto, Turner, Monet, or Manet) but may also represent them with a distinct style that is about the artwork itself rather than the world. For example, when we compare Turner and Monet's paintings of the Houses of Parliament and the Grand Canal, we can see that they not only represent the same objects, but also do so with such distinct styles that it may be argued that the two Turners and two Monets resemble each other more than they resemble paintings of the same objects by the other painter. Arguably, historiographic connoisseurs may similarly distinguish between historiographic narratives according to their artistic styles. In Ankersmit's philosophy, the empirical evidence confers on historiographic narratives only *adequacy*. Contradictory but equally adequate, narratives are founded on the same "observations." Like art, historiographic narratives are neither true nor false, so they do not result from reasoning.

Composing historiography in Ankersmit's philosophy is analogous to baking an apple pie (strudel): Obviously, the process begins with apple pickers choosing which apples are ripe or raw and which are rotten. The apple pickers are necessary and their work is important; the greatest chef cannot bake from rotten apples. But once the ripe apples are brought to the kitchen, the cooks can display their genius. Cooking apprentices study the kitchen and not the orchard. Likewise, historians pick and choose the "ripe" facts and discard the forged or unreliable ones. They bring the collected "facts" to the historiographic "kitchen" where historians conceptualize, slice and combine them with added explanations, value judgements, and a pinch of theory, then pour them into readymade narrative pans to give them structure and form, and slide them into the narrative oven to bake together, until ready for public consumption. Different cooks may make different dishes and give them different tastes in different shapes from the same apples. It is ridiculous to reason for or against pies unless the apples are rotten: *De gustibus non est disputandum.*

Still, researching and writing historiography is not analogous to baking pies. There are no ripe and ready facts that can be observed in the archives and collected without reasoning. The archive is not made of apple-like distinct atomic observational facts, ready to be baked in the historian's narrative workshop. Historiographic "facts" are inferred from the evidence in a process of historiographic reasoning. The final product of historiographic research may have the form of a narrative. But that final form is the *superstructure* of historiography, as Goldstein (1976) put it; its substance is reasoned from the evidence.

5 Historiographic Reasoning in Unified Science

It may be argued that indeed historiography reasons from the evidence, but that this reasoning is indistinguishable from scientific reasoning in general, because historiography is a branch of a unified science. This treatise would then be redundant since any introduction to the philosophy of science should cover similar grounds.

Murray Murphey (2009) proposed that the relations between historiography and evidence are just like those between scientific theories and evidence. "Historical Knowledge is a theoretical construct to account for presently observable data" (6). Murphey (1973, 16) famously likened George Washington to the electron, "an entity postulated for the purpose of giving coherence to our present experience, ... each is unobservable by us." Scientific theories model unobservable nature; historiography models the unobservable past. Historiography, like scientific theories, is well justified when it can explain all the relevant evidence for its subject, is consistent with other parts of historiography, and is able to explain new evidence (Murphey 2009, 11).

Historiography indeed shares with scientific theories the postulation of entities or events that are unobservable and must be inferred from evidence. But there are a few differences between the electron and George Washington: The electron is an abstract type – it has neither space nor time, President Washington was a particular token who lived from 1732 to 1799 in one place for a limited time. To grasp the difference between types and tokens, consider that if we have the same *type* of parents, we belong to the same species; if we have the same *token* parents, we are siblings; if two students submit the same type of article, they wrote on similar topics; if they submit the same token article, one of them is a plagiarist. Different laboratories can conjure different particular *tokens* of scientific types, like electrons, and conduct experiments on them. By contrast, George Washington occurred only once; laboratories cannot replicate tokens of George Washington.

Murphey (2009, 151) argued that replication is as possible in historiography as in science because historians can reinspect the same public evidence. However, "replications" in the historical sciences are of observations of the same *tokens* (e.g. the same documents in the same archives). Replication in the theoretical sciences is of *different tokens* of the same evidentiary types to support generalizations about the types, for example of different token electrons in different laboratories (see Van Fraassen 1980, 123). These different goals necessitate different types of reasoning.

6 Historiographic Reasoning as Social Science

An enlightenment tradition has considered historiography an applied social science, and the social sciences applied psychology. Hume and J. S. Mill thought there were universal laws of human nature that historians should apply to understand history. Marx's theory was interpreted by many as political economics applied to historiography. Taken to an extreme, the concept of historiography as applied social science may lead to the idea that applied historiography can form the basis of social-historical engineering and a new type of technocratic politics, run by social engineers, as the St. Simonians advocated, and Isaac Asimov brilliantly explored in his science fiction *Foundations* trilogy (Tucker 2021). If historiography is applied social science, this treatise is redundant, since introductions to the philosophy and methodology of the social sciences should fulfil the same purpose. Indeed, years ago

I complained to a philosopher friend that there were no job advertisements for philosophers of history or historiography. He advised me to apply for positions in philosophy of the social sciences. I replied that I am philosophically committed to distinguishing the philosophy of historiography from the philosophy of the social sciences. My friend retorted: "Well, they would not know it!"

The historical sciences are interested in token events, whereas the social sciences are interested in theories about types of events. For example, revolution is a type. The French Revolution and the Russian Revolution were tokens of this type. Revolution as a type does not exist in space and time. The French and Russian revolutions had a beginning, middle, and an end and they happened in particular geographical locations. Historians have attempted to infer knowledge of the French Revolution from evidence that preserved information about it. By contrast, the social sciences attempt to generate theories about the causes and effects of revolutions. Social science theories about types like "revolution" do not have to be about their tokens. Vice versa, tokens like the French Revolution can illustrate discussions of their types, but cannot confirm or refute theories of revolution. If social science theories are confused with historiography, as shorthand for collections of historical tokens, for example, a theory of revolutions as a generalization of what took place in the French, Russian, Chinese, and other revolutions, the social science theories are forced into a zero-value sum game of three cognitive values of theories, scope, accuracy, and simplicity: Scope comes at the expense of accuracy because to fit more than a single token event, the theory must become vague. For example, if a theory of revolution attempts to fit historical revolutions, each additional revolution will force the theory to become vaguer not to contradict the particular properties of the marginally added revolution. If a simple theory attempts to apply to a broader scope of historical cases, it will accumulate exceptions and anomalies and will be forced to become complex to explain them. If a complex theory tries to become simpler, it will have to retreat from some of its scope, or become vaguer. Graphically, this zero sum game of total cognitive value can be represented on a graph where the horizontal line represents the cognitive values of accuracy and scope at opposite poles, and the vertical line represents the opposite poles of complexity and simplicity (see Figure 1). Applied to historiography, social science theories can move either on the horizontal line, broaden scope by becoming vaguer, less informative, or become more accurate, more informative, by narrowing the scope, or broaden scope at the expense of simplicity.

As long as social science theories remain on the level of types, they can score highly on all the preceding cognitive values. When applied to historiography the

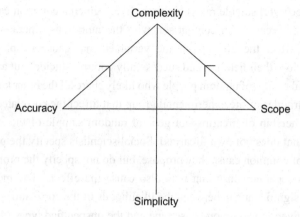

Figure 1 Historiography as applied social science suffers from a zero sum game of total cognitive value.

total cognitive values of theories is lower, and there are trade-offs between the values of the cognitive values when rise in one necessitates fall in another.

Social science hypotheses typically connect types of causes with correlated types of effects. Historical token causes and effects that exist in space and time transmute into theoretical types of causal relations by averaging causal effects. For example (Van Dam 2024), there is a correlation between higher-than-average rates of voting for the Republican Party in the United States, higher than average rates of hearing loss, and higher than average rates of successful suicide attempts. The social sciences attempt to find a common type of cause or causes for these correlations between these three types, Republican voting, hearing loss, and death by suicide. Can you guess the answer?

The causal explanation for the preceding correlations is higher than average rates of ownership of firearms. Gun owners tend to vote for the Party that protects the second amendment right of gun owners to bear arms, and they tend to lose their hearing because without protection the noise of shooting damages hearing. Though the rate of Republicans who *attempt* to commit suicide is similar to that of the general American population, those who attempt to commit suicide by *shooting* themselves have a considerably higher rate of success than those who try to commit suicide by other means that can be reversed, such as taking an overdose of pills. Social scientists measure *averages* of these putative types of causes and effects, not individual sequences of causes and effects. In the real world it is probably quite rare to find gun owners who cannot hear well, but still vote Republicans, and then shoot themselves dead, just as there is a vanishing number of families with 2.2 children. Social scientists prove that the correlations between types of effects (Republican voting, hearing loss, and successful suicide rates) are more likely given a common cause type (ownership of firearms) in comparison with the numerous separate types of causes that affect the effects (all the variables that cause people to vote Republican, lose their hearing, and successfully commit suicide) but are shared with a control group (of random people who likely share all the other known and unknown variables of the experimental group that affect the correlated effects, save for ownership of firearms – a general random sample of the American population that does not own firearms). Social scientists specify the properties of the type of common cause they propose, but do not specify the properties of the types of separate cause that may also cause the effects. The method for achieving a significant gap between the likelihoods of the correlations between the effects given the common cause type and the unspecified types of separate causes is the random assignment of members to two populations to make them nearly identically affected by the same types of causal factors except for the "treatment" common cause type that all the members of one group share and none of the members of the other (control) group are affected by (ownership of firearms in the preceding example). This is comparable to experiments that determine the efficacy of new medicine by giving it to one randomly assigned group while giving a placebo to another. Significant differences between the two populations are likely then to be the result of that common cause type, or "treatment." The "Neyman–Rubin method" of random assignment to two groups is practiced across the sciences, for example in pharmacology, medicine, and agronomy (Tucker 2012, 2014). In nonexperimental settings, social sciences use statistical techniques instead of random assignment to hold different variables constant while measuring others. Social scientists may then conduct multivariate regression analyses that generate equations and multi-equation models, and causal maps that measure strengths of causal influences.

Historians by contrast would find evidence for how owning firearms affected individuals, and social historians may amalgamate those findings to identify a trend. Historians do not randomize or conduct regression analysis that is about types rather than token events.

The goals and methods of the historical sciences are mirror images of those of the social sciences: Historiography is interested in inferring *token common origin*, such as a historical event, of information-preserving evidence, such as the testimonies of eyewitnesses to that event. As I outline next, historiography compares the probabilities that correlated evidence such as coherent independent testimonies preserve information from some *common origin* whose properties are *unknown*, with the probability that the evidence preserved information from separate *token origins* whose properties are *specified*. Note the contrast with the social sciences where the inference is of a common cause *type* whose properties are *specified*, while the properties of the numerous alternative possible *separate causes*, shared with the control group, are *not specified*. Social scientists use statistical randomization techniques to prove the causal relevance of common cause types. But historians try to prove that the information preserved in the evidence is more likely given a common origin that transmitted the shared or coherent information, than given separate origins, *using information theories* and tracing the information channels, as shown next.

7 Bayesian Foundations of Historiographic Reasoning

Try to think of historical events as information "explosions" that send information waves in all directions. (Lewis 1979; Cleland 2002, 2009) Most of the information decays quickly or mixes with noise: Memories fade or get missed with later memories and testimonies; written reports are destroyed, discarded, and disappear; witnesses die without leaving testimonial records, and so on. A small fraction of that information is preserved in historiographic evidence. History is a collection of *origins* of information signals that transmit encoded information signals to present *receivers*, the evidence (see Kosso 2001). Historiographic reasoning is displayed when historians decode the information in the evidence to infer the existence of its origins and some of their properties. There are numerous types of information signals, codes, and transmission channels such as documents, material remains, DNA, and languages. Information transmissions supervene on physical channels: Identical information may be transmitted orally, in documents, in different languages, in prose or verse, on paper, papyrus, or skins, electronically, via radio, telegraph, digitally, and so on. During transmission, information is in a period of *latency* when it is not expressed. Information signals are mixed with varying levels of *noise* and have different levels of *equivocation*, loss of signal. Information transmissions have *reliabilities* or *fidelities*, the ratio of preserved information at the end of the process of transmission to the information that is transmitted from the origins. For example, oral traditions are much less reliable than personal diaries because they preserve less information from their origins.

A treatise devoted to historiographic reasoning must clarify, first and foremost, the conditional relations between evidence and historiography, how historians infer probable knowledge of the past from information-preserving evidence in the present? The rule named after Bayes (that was actually introduced first by Laplace) has been used often to explicate the relations between evidence and hypotheses in realms as different as astronomy, code breaking, resource geology, and the philosophy of science (Bertsch-McGrayne 2011). It gives a clear formal answer to the question: How evidence affects degrees of belief (credence)? Bayesian reasoning is already used explicitly in some historical sciences such as phylogeny (Felsenstein 2004, 288–306), archaeology (Buck et al. 1996), cosmology (Hobson 2010), and historical linguistics (Greenhill et al. 2020) to justify inferences of probable knowledge of history. In the historiography of the human past, Richard Carrier (2012, 2014) attempted to apply Bayesian reasoning to inferences from the texts of the New Testament. In the philosophy of the historical sciences, Elliott Sober (e.g. 1988), has applied Bayesian probability for understanding phylogenic reasoning, as Wallach (2018) applied for understanding inferences in archaeological science.

Most practicing historians undoubtedly have never heard of Bayes' rule, know little about probability theory, and therefore have not considered whether or not they have been practicing Bayesian methods. Nevertheless, most historians usually follow Bayes' rule tacitly, without being aware of it. The relation between the inferences historians make and Bayes' rule is comparable to the relations between natural speakers of languages, who have not studied them, and the rules of grammar they usually follow tacitly, without being able to articulate them. If somebody violates the rules of grammar, other speakers would notice it, and could correct the mistake, without necessarily being able to articulate the grammatical rules they enforce.

I state first Bayes' rule and what it means for explicating historiographic reasoning. I write the following with readers who have not been exposed to formal approaches to epistemology in mind. I promise this is not difficult, is extremely enlightening, and can actually be fun! So, please don't cheat; read on rather than skip the best parts!

In the equation:

$$\Pr(H|E\,\&\,B)=[\Pr(E|H\,\&\,B) \times \Pr(H|B)] : \Pr(E|B)$$

Pr stands for the probability of . . .

H (Hypothesis) stands for any claim about history that we wish to examine in light of evidence, for example, the hypothesis that there were transpacific contacts and exchanges between Polynesian and South American societies and cultures before Europeans discovered the New World and Polynesia.

E (Evidence) stands for *new* evidence that preserves information from the past and may be conditionally relevant for the probability of the hypothesis, for example, the discovery of potato tubers that Polynesians cultivated before coming into contact with Europeans in the material remains of Captain Cook's expedition to Polynesia.

B stands for background knowledge, historiography known *prior to the new evidence E*. For example, all that was known about the cultures of

Polynesia and South America before the discovery of potato tubers in Captain Cook's collection.

The vertical line | should be read as "given that," as in the probability of one thing given another thing, such as the probability that Polynesians cultivated potatoes before coming into contact with Europeans given the discovery of the potato tubers.

So:

Pr(H|E&B) reads the probability of the hypothesis given the new evidence and all that has been known before its discovery. This measures the *posterior probability* of a hypothesis, after the new evidence is taken into consideration, along with the background knowledge known before the discovery of the new evidence, for example, the probability that there was a transpacific exchange given everything that has been known about ancient Polynesia and South America as well as the new evidence about the Polynesian potato. This is the side of the equation historians attempt to solve: what is the *posterior probability* of a historiographic hypothesis, considering new evidence and everything known previously.

Pr(H|B) reads as the probability of the hypothesis given the background knowledge that was known prior to the discovery of the new evidence, it is the *prior* probability of the hypothetical claim conditional on what was known before the new evidence. For example, given everything known about the navigational and seafaring technologies of the Polynesian and pre-Columbian cultures of South America, the probability of a transpacific exchange was rather low.

Pr(E|H) reads the probability of the evidence given the hypothesis; assuming the hypothesis, how likely is the evidence? The *likelihood* of the new evidence assumes (without proving) that the hypothesis in question is true. It measures the probability of the evidence as a function of the hypothesis. For example, if it is assumed (purely hypothetically) that there was a transpacific exchange, how probable is the ancient Polynesians' cultivation of potatoes? This likelihood is high.

Pr(E|B) = [Pr(E|H) × Pr(H|B)] + [Pr(E|−H) × Pr(−H|B)] expresses the *expectedness*, the probability of the evidence whether or not the hypothesis is true. For example, how probable is it that the ancient Polynesians cultivated potatoes whether or not there was a transpacific exchange. It read: The probability of the evidence given everything we knew before its discovery is equal to the probability of the evidence assuming the hypothesis multiplied by its prior probability before the discovery of the evidence plus the probability of the evidence assuming that the hypothesis is not true multiplied by the prior probability that the hypothesis is not true.

Finally, the pivotal computation: the *posterior probability* of the hypothesis given the evidence and background information, is the ratio of the *likelihood* of the evidence given the hypothesis multiplied by the *prior* probability of the hypothesis, to the *expectedness* probability of the occurrence of the evidence whether or not the hypothesis is true:

$$[\Pr(E|H) \times \Pr(H|B)]: \Pr(E|B)$$

Which reads: The probability of the evidence assuming the hypothesis is true multiplied by the prior probability of the hypothesis before the discovery of the evidence divided by the probability of the evidence whether or not the hypothesis is true. For example, historians evaluate the probability that there was transpacific exchange on the basis of everything known prior to the discovery of Cook's Polynesian potato tubers. Then, assuming there was a transpacific exchange, how probable is the discovery of potato tubers that were cultivated in Polynesia prior to the arrival of Europeans. Finally, historians divide the prior probability multiplied by the likelihood, by the expectedness, the probability that the potato tubers would be found whether or not there was a transpacific exchange. Another way to imagine the meaning of posterior probability is to imagine all the possible worlds where potato tubers would be found among Captain Cook's collections and ask in what portion of those worlds there was a transpacific exchange in comparison with all the worlds in which the Polynesians cultivated potatoes without a transpacific exchange. This important ratio measures the *significance* of the evidence for justifying the hypothesis, how strong is the conditional justification of the hypothesis by the evidence. If it is implausible that potato tubers would be found in Captain Cook's collections without a previous transpacific exchange, this evidence is decisive. The most useful evidence for historians is surprising, unexpected, for hypotheses that have low prior probabilities because such evidence raises dramatically the posterior probability of the hypothesis because there is no other explanation for the evidence. For example, the prior probability that there was a transpacific exchange of crops between Polynesia and South America, of crossing the Pacific Ocean from South America to Polynesia with premodern native American or Polynesian seafaring technology, without a compass, was quite low. But since the potato is native to the Andes region, it had to somehow get to Polynesia from South America, and it is probably too far for currents, birds, and other accidents to make the transmission of the potato likely. The premodern potato cultivation then is surprising and therefore *crucial* evidence for premodern Pacific intercontinental travel, improbable though it may have seemed prior to the discovery of the evidence.

A common objection to the application of Bayesian models that may seem particularly appropriate to historiography, is that there is no universal method for quantifying likelihood, expectedness, and so on in nonquantitative fields that do not measure variables. But for Bayes' rule to be useful for historiography, the quantitative values can be "fuzzy," have ranges of values. In the example about the Polynesian potato and pre-Columbian transpacific exchange, historians need to agree just that the probability of the Polynesian potato without humans crossing the Pacific from South America to Polynesia is negligible. If so, the posterior probability of the Pacific exchange is extremely high. How high? High enough. It does not matter exactly where it is on the range between 0.9 and 0.999. Fuzzy numbers can be assessed subjectively, but not arbitrarily. Experts estimate probabilities tacitly and have a range of conclusions that tend to converge when the evidence is decisive. Their estimates do not have to be identical, as long as they are close enough to each other, to decide whether the posterior probabilities are high enough to be considered knowledge, or not. If they are close enough, a consensus about the posterior probabilities will follow. In cases when the evidence is less decisive, there may be disagreements about posterior probabilities. Historians may attempt to break such probabilistic ties by looking for and discovering new evidence.

Historiography is a progressive science. People who confuse history with historiography may conclude that since history cannot be changed, historiography is fixed; or vice versa that since historiography changes, so does history. But progress in historiography usually follows the discovery of surprising new evidence. Bayes' rule explains why and how. It explains the practices of historians who search assiduously for new evidence to decide historiographic hypotheses. The discovery of new evidence may result from luck or grit, or it may follow the discovery or application of new information theories that direct historians where to look for surprising evidence. For example, Ranke innovated in using state and diplomatic archives to discover reliable evidence that led to his rewriting of European historiography. Marc Bloch (1961) innovated in using the shapes of fields as evidence to infer the historical economies that generated them. Demographic historians innovated in using parish registries to generate data bases (e.g Razi 1980). Art historians innovated in discovering everyday life through their artistic depictions (Burke 2019). Scientific innovations like DNA analysis allowed historians to extract more information from known evidence. For example, by distinguishing which of the Dead Sea scrolls were written on sheepskin and which on cow skin, historians were able to determine which scrolls were imported since cows cannot live around the Dead Sea, though sheep can (Anava et al. 2020). Court records that documented testimonies of illiterate people, albeit from the perspective of the scribes who recorded them, offered surprising information about the lives and beliefs of subaltern populations and the limited reach of Christianity among the lower classes (Ginzburg 1980). Theories of monetary inflation and deflation interpret ancient "shaving" of coins that debased them, or coins where noble metals were mixed with varying amounts of base metals, as forms of deflation in relation to a metal standard (De Cecco 1985).

8 Transmission vs. Generation of Historiographic Knowledge

Historiography is a function of its evidence. The functional relations between historiographic outputs and evidential inputs may be divided into *epistemic transmission* and *epistemic generation.* "Knowledge generation is about producing knowledge, in the sense of bringing it into existence. Knowledge transmission is about distributing knowledge that already exists" (Greco 2020, 1). Transmission of knowledge requires epistemic inputs to be sufficiently justified to be considered knowledge, and the transmission process must be sufficiently *reliable* to preserve these justifications. The degree of reliability in transmission is measured by how much of the grounds for knowledge that were transmitted from the input reached the output. Obviously, grounds for knowledge must be present in the inputs to be *transmitted* to their outputs. For example, the inputs for ancient historiography are in many cases themselves outputs of long chains of historiographic inputs and outputs where information was transmitted with varying levels of reliability. Some of these inputs are not sufficiently justified to be considered knowledge and hence cannot transmit it to historiographic outputs. Other such inputs have sufficient grounds for knowledge, for example, eyewitness reports.

When knowledge is *transmitted* from a single input, a simple and straightforward application of Bayes' rule implies that historians assess the prior probability of the transmitted knowledge, multiply it by the assessed *reliability* of the transmitting evidence given the knowledge, and divide the result by the expectedness of the evidence irrespective of whether it transmits knowledge or not. Generally, criteria for estimating likelihoods-reliabilities of historiographic testimonial evidence, whether the information they transmit likely preserves information transmitted from the historical event(s), include estimates of the biases of the testimonial-evidential source, its motivations for transmitting the information, its expectations prior to receiving the information it testifies to, the relevant knowledge or expertise it possessed about the contents of the testimony (e.g. whether a medical diagnosis is delivered by a witness with medical training), the level of access the witness had to the reported information (e.g. whether the witness was present at the events they report about), the evidential source's sensory and recall abilities, its reputation, record for accuracy on this topic, whether the evidence is a primary source or a secondary/relaying source, whether the information was modified or distorted if it was transmitted through secondary sources, and the internal consistency of the information (see Irwin & Mandel 2019, 515–516).

Historiography, however, does not have to rely on the transmission of knowledge because historiographic reasoning can also *generate* it through epistemic processes that generate epistemic probable outputs from unreliable inputs. Epistemic generation is a functional relation between epistemic outputs and inputs whereby the outputs have stronger epistemic grounds than their inputs. The most important epistemic generation is of knowledge from inputs whose epistemic grounds are insufficient for justifying knowledge.

9 Generative Historiographic Reasoning in Three Stages

Historiography often *generates* historiographic knowledge as an output of a process of reasoning. Coherent and independent evidential inputs that are individually too unreliable to transmit knowledge can generate knowledge together by demonstrating that the coherence of the information signals they carry does not result from dependency or shared biases, and is not random. This generative process of reasoning has three stages that consecutively separate information from noise, trace the information back to its historical origin, and infer properties of the origin – the historical event or process that sent the information signals to the evidence. First, historians prove that detailed and coherent evidential inputs are more likely to have had some common historical origin than different origins. Second, if it is probable that the evidence had some common origin, historians infer the information channels that connected past events to present evidence. This tracing of information flows serves to ascertain the independence or dependence of the evidence. Finally, historians attempt to generate knowledge of properties of the historical origins of the evidence from independent evidence.

The process of generation of historiographic knowledge begins with coherent information stored by units of evidence such as documents, material remains, DNA, and so on. Information is distinct from propositional content of evidence because some propositionally incoherent testimonies can carry coherent information, for example, when a proposition is ironic or conveys the opposite of its propositional content by adding to it some information that is obviously false, for example, when smart witnesses who are coerced to "confess" include in their "confession" blatant falsities about fictional characters or dead people to discredit their own testimonies. Some testimonies may be "encoded" and require a "cipher" to decode the information signals they carry. Detectives, historians, and anthropologists specialize in generating coherent information from such propositionally *incoherent* testimonies. Vice versa, coherences do not have to be propositional, for example, when there is systematic correspondence between languages, DNA sequences, and artistic and architectural styles and techniques such as Greco-Buddhist sculptures that preserve information about original cultural contacts and exchanges between Hellenic and Indian artists. More particular forms of information coherence include narrative coherence and colligation (see Kuukkanen 2015). A sequence of temporally ordered inputs may form a *coherent narrative*. In a coherent narrative, the information that part of the narrative conveys increases the probabilities of the information conveyed by other inputs. For example, if each evidential source records the presence of an army at a particular space at a particular time and the form of transportation is known, together, they can generate a coherent narrative of a campaign. Colligation demonstrates that evidence forms a part of a coherent whole such as an artistic style or an intellectual movement. For example, various aspects of the Renaissance may be colligated as being coherently humanistic, placing the human, rather than the divine, in the center of the universe.

Coherence of preserved *information*, in Shannon (1964) classical sense of information as "diminishing uncertainty," is common to all the diverse types of coherence that initiate the generation of historiographic knowledge. Some testimonial evidence may preserve information in coherent propositional contents. Other evidence may preserve encoded information that requires decoding first with the help of information theories. Informational coherence is the degree of coherence between the information signals that epistemic inputs carry. For example, if there is a high statistical correlation between properties P and Q (like literacy and a centralized tax collecting state) in history and if one historical source testified that A was P (e.g. that a population was literate), and another witness testifies that A was Q (e.g. the population was ruled by a centralized state and bureaucracy), the testimonies strongly cohere and are useful for the inference of a literate population in a centralized state.

Once historians discover evidential coherence, they ask whether the coherence results from the preservation of information transmitted from some common historical origin, or whether the coherence has other reasons or has no reason and was random. For example, do the coherences Greco-Buddhist art displays with Greek and Buddhist arts preserve evidence for intercultural contact and hybridization, or could they have developed in Northern India without contacts between the Buddhist and Hellenic civilizations? By contrast, large pyramids were built in ancient Egypt, Mesopotamia, and Mesoamerica. Do they preserve information about a common origin, or is there a different reason for the coherence, such as the constraint of gravity that forces large buildings, before columns and arches were invented, to have had the shape of a pyramid to avoid collapsing under their own weight? Does the coherent number of seven days in a week across many cultures reflect a common (Sumerian) origin, or different origins such as the universal need to divide the universal natural number of days in a lunar month to fit to human labor and rest rhythms? Do coherences between language families preserve information about common origins, or are they random? Do historical testimonies agree because of a common historical origin or because the coherent information served their independent interests? Since the *common* and *different* information origins of evidential coherencies are exhaustive and mutually exclusive, the improbability of one implies the probability of the other.

When the gap between the likelihoods of the evidence given the common and different origins hypotheses is sufficiently large, quantitative precision is unnecessary; probabilistic fuzziness is just as good. For example, information-rich pieces of evidence from several sources about historical events and processes that detail what happened, how, when, where, and so on, probably share some common origins (that do not have to be the events they describe, but can also be a common source of disinformation) because randomly coherent detailed testimonies are unlikely, nor is it probable that different interests could explain the precise and detailed coherences. By contrast, generic, information-poor, coherent testimonies may have no common origin, but reflect common biases such as blaming a traditional scapegoat, the historiographic equivalent to "the butler did it" in classical detective stories, or just be random. The likelihoods of testimonies that convey coherent information given different sources of information is assessed by considering the various advantages – material, psychological, and so on – that the testimonies may have conferred on the historical testifiers. This requires background knowledge about their circumstances and social contexts. Testimonies that were disadvantageous for the witnesses or at least had no value for them, such as deathbed confessions, are not likely given different origins and so probably preserve information from a common origin. The likelihood of testimony that conflicts with the interests or biases of witnesses is low; the likelihood of a set of such testimonies, given different origins, is vanishing. The odds of random coherence depend on how information rich is the coherence. The more information rich is the coherence, the lower are the odds that the coherence emerged randomly, and vice versa. For example, the coherence in the sounds of individual words in different languages is information poor and can emerge randomly. Systematic coherence in grammatical rules and sets of words is more information rich and hence less likely to emerge randomly.

Each additional coherent evidence can increase the probability of a common origin by decreasing the posterior probability of its only alternative, different origins. Still, since a small number of information-rich and surprising coherent evidential inputs is usually sufficient for decreasing the probability of different origins to negligible, historians do not need more than a few evidential inputs to determine common origins. The historian need not bother then to search for additional coherent evidence when the probability that the evidential inputs had different origins is already negligible. For example, if there are three of four coherent testimonies to a historical event, the fifth and sixth coherent testimonies will not add to the probability of what they cohere about, and so are redundant.

The prior probability of some common origin of coherent evidential inputs is estimated according to the probability that the information signals that led to the evidential inputs could have intersected. For example, the information signals that generated Greco-Buddhist art may well have intersected as a result of the previously known Macedonian campaign in Northern India. The information signals that generated the pyramids of the Aztecs and Babylonians probably could not have intersected because of geographical and historical distance.

To sum up. according to the Bayesian theorem, in the first stage of inference, the prior probability of the hypothesis of some common origin of the evidence is multiplied by the likelihood of the coherent evidence given that it had some common origin, and divided by the expectedness – the likelihood of the coherent evidential inputs whether or not they had a common origin. If the coherent evidence is unlikely given different origins, the posterior probability of the common origin hypothesis is high, and the process of generation of historiographic knowledge proceeds to the next stage.

If the posterior probability of some common historical origin of coherent evidence is high, alternative information channels or flow nets that connect that common origin with the evidence need to be evaluated against each other. The most important question historians need to answer about these channels is whether the coherent evidential units are independent of each other. Evidential independence means the absence of information flows between the evidential inputs or the information channels that connected them to their common origin. Epistemic inputs that retransmit information from other channels are dependent on their sources; otherwise, they are independent.

Coherence of evidential inputs is necessary, but insufficient, for the generation of knowledge. The inputs must also be epistemically independent; otherwise, coherence may reflect transmissions of information between the evidential inputs or the information channels that led to them (Bovens and Hartmann 2003, 15). It may be possible to trace back the information transmitting processes extending backward from each unit of evidence "genealogically" (Jardine 2008, 170–171). Historians attempt to track the information channels backward from the evidence to discover where they intersected. For example, testimonies of eyewitnesses who could not have, or were unlikely to have, communicated with each other, such as reports of rivals, are likely to be independent. Independence is in relation to a common origin, about the information signals and channels between the origin and the evidence.

If the evidential inputs transferred information to each other, but also received information independently from a common origin or origins, they may be used for the generation of historiographic knowledge only if historians can separate the independent signals from the dependent noise. For example, textual criticism detects information signals that indicate the temporal-historical and geographical origins of parts of composite documents such as the Judeo-Christian scriptures or Homeric poems that can then be analyzed into their constituent documents that can infer their origins. Internal contradictions, gaps in narratives, parts that are inconsistent with the alleged identity of the author, discontinuities in vocabulary, grammar, syntax, style, conceptual framework, and implicit values that can be compared with other documents whose time and space are known, can be used to distinguish information flows and infer common origins (Grafton 1990).

If evidential inputs are coherent, independent, and have low prior probabilities, for example because they are very detailed, the coherences likely result from preservation of information from some common origin. The remaining task then is to use this coherent information to infer properties of that common origin. In the final stage of the generation of historiographic knowledge, historiographic reasoning generates knowledge of properties of the common origins of coherent and independent evidential inputs.

Prior probabilities of the generated knowledge of history reflect coherence with established historiographic knowledge. In simple cases of coherence of propositional contents between evidential inputs, it may be easy to infer properties of their common origin from the propositional contents. More sophisticated inferences use nonpropositional types of information coherences. For example, the discovery that in carnivorous societies, rise in the disposable income of the poor working class creates a signal in the form of greater consumption of meat can lead to using correlations between rises in meat consumption in different markets to infer changes in the standard of living of the poor (see the ensuing debate about Thompson's method in Taylor 1975). The various indicators that economic historians use to measure economic performance, such as data about the movements of freight trains, are all founded on information generalizations to extract information about common origins. Information-preserving coherences between forms of artefacts, shapes of fields, artistic styles, languages, and so on can infer properties of their common origins, economic structures, technologies, migrations, and intercultural contacts.

If there are incoherent testimonies, investigators group the testimonies in sets that share coherent information and follow the preceding three stages to infer their posterior probabilities. If there is a single dissenting testimony, its reliability is crucial; low reliability can discount the testimony. Otherwise, the output with the highest posterior probability is more competitive than its alternatives. If the posterior probabilities of several inconsistent epistemic outputs about the properties of common origins are close to each other, they are underdetermined.

10 History of Historiographic Reasoning

Historiographic reasoning has a history. It may be divided, following the distinction between the transmission and generation of knowledge of history, into three stages. (I do apologize to the reader for introducing yet another tripartite historical periodization, but the historiographic evidence forces my hand.) First, there was no knowledge of history because knowledge of the past was neither transmitted nor generated. There were unreliable myths, stories, and traditions. Probable historiographic knowledge appeared in history when historians developed methods for the evaluation of evidential reliability of transmitted information from the past, chose the more reliable evidential inputs, and discarded the unreliable ones. Thirdly, a scientific-historiographic revolution that culminated in Ranke's paradigm enabled the *generation* of historiographic knowledge from epistemic inputs that were not necessarily reliable enough to transmit knowledge. The transmission and generation of knowledge from testimonies in courts of law went through identical and simultaneous phases that coincided with the evolution of historiographic reasoning. Thucydides "was writing for an audience used to weighing up competing oral testimonies, and not as a modern historian weighing up a wide variety of different sorts of sources. He was seeking to produce an account that transcended the partial narratives typical of the courtroom. Thucydides says little about how he went about the task of analysing conflicting claims from eyewitnesses" (Rood 2006, 237). Thucydides and his classical successors sought to infer the reliabilities of witnesses, especially when they disagreed, and practised source criticism, partly by considering biases, as in court, but did not seek to *generate* new historiographic knowledge from independent testimonial inputs, as Ranke and modern historians would.

The transition from myth to historiography, the birth of critical historiography with Herodotus and its achievement of an ancient zenith with Thucydides, are well-known and covered in most introductions to historiography, so I have nothing new, smart, or interesting to say about it. The groundbreaking transition from transmission of reliable historiographic knowledge to its generation has not been recognized and therefore deserves meticulous attention.

In medieval Roman law, the strength of legal proofs was described in terms of fractions. "[T]he corroborative testimony of two unimpeachable eyewitnesses constituted a complete proof" (Daston 1988, 42). If only less reliable witnesses, whose reliability was represented by lower fractions, were available, their testimonies could add up to a "full proof," if there were more and enough of them. This was also Thucydides' and the best of pre-Rankean historiography's approach to receiving transmitted knowledge of history from testimonies. They reasoned by inquiring after the reliability of the witnesses and sought reliable coherent testimonies that "added up."

The article about *probabilité* in the *Encyclopédie* of 1765, written probably by Diderot, represents an intermediary phase between ancient transmission and modern generation of knowledge of history. The article described how two witnesses with the same reliability can *generate* knowledge more reliable than their own with the following formula:

The posterior probability of two coherent testimtextnies

$$= 1 - (1-\text{reliability rate})^2$$

For example, the posterior probability of what two testimonies with a 0.9 reliability agree on is $0.99 = 1 - (1 - 0.9)^2$. If their reliabilities are lower, 0.5, $1 - (1 - 0.5)^2 = 0.75$, and so on. When there are more testimonies, the leap from individual reliability to posterior probabilities is larger. For example, if there are three rather than two coherent testimonies with 0.5 reliabilities: $1 - (1 - 0.5)^3 = 0.875$, and so on. This is the first quantitative representation of the *generation of knowledge* in world history since the resulting posterior probabilities can be considerably higher than the individual reliabilities of each of the testimonies. Still, the article did not take into consideration the effect of prior probabilities on posterior probabilities that explain why surprising testimonies of low prior probability that cohere generate more probable epistemic outputs than expected unsurprising coherent testimonies, because the evidence is unlikely if the hypothesis is false. Most significantly, the article did not mention the independence of the witnesses as a necessary condition for the generation of knowledge (Daston 1988, 318–320).

All the elements of the generation of knowledge from multiple evidential inputs came into place in Laplace's treatise on probabilities from 1796. Laplace (1840, 136–156) formalized the generation of knowledge from multiple testimonies by fully applying what would be unjustly known as Bayes' rather than Laplace's theorem. He demonstrated that in a fair draw of one from one hundred numbers (i.e. the prior probability of each number is 1:100), when two witnesses report that the same number was drawn and their reliabilities are respectively 0.9 and 0.7, they generate a posterior probability of considerably higher probability, 2079/2080. Laplace recognized that low prior probabilities increase the posterior probability of what independent testimonies agree on. Laplace demonstrated then mathematically that knowledge can be *generated* even from *unreliable* but *independent* testimonial inputs. Arguably, this was the high watermark of a scientific revolution in Kuhn's (1996) sense.

The enlightenment philosophers who developed probabilistic methods for the generation of knowledge from testimonies were interested in a probabilistic foundation for institutional reform of jury systems to maximize the odds for correct verdicts. They hoped to apply their theories to rationalize the judicial system. These enlightenment aspirations for rationalizing reforms of society and the judicial system were cut off, not to say decapitated, by the devolution of the Revolution into rule by terror, whose main rationalizing achievement was not jury reform but the invention of the guillotine. I did not find evidence that the enlightenment philosophers proceeded to apply their theoretical innovations to reform the generation of historiographic knowledge from the testimonies of the dead. The generation of knowledge from multiple independent historical testimonies was introduced at the same time, the second half of the eighteenth century, but not at the same place, France, but in German-speaking universities by academics who were considered at the time "philologists" whether they practiced their trade in linguistics, theology, classics, or later history departments. I have not discovered a "smoking gun" proof that the philologists were influenced by the French enlightenment philosophers' concern with probabilities, testimonies, and juries, or vice versa, whether the enlightenment philosophers were thinking of theorizing the research methods of the German philologists. Until further research is conducted to look for evidence that would prove or disprove such influences, they are between the possible and the plausible.

The first materials the philologists attempted to use as evidential inputs, the Old and New Testaments and a bit later the Greek and Latin classics, were significantly more difficult, less "user friendly," than the archival documents Ranke would use a generation or two later. The generation of knowledge requires coherent and independent, evidentiary inputs. Ranke's archived documents were usually such independent and reliable evidential inputs. Ranke could quite easily ascertain their independence and the origin of their information. By contrast, the New and Old Testaments and Homer's epic poems are composites of documents that were written in different places at different times, but edited together later. Consequently, much of the work the philologists had to perform was to analyze the composites into their distinct documentary components before trying to use them as epistemic inputs to infer their genealogies and whether or not they were independent and useful for generating some knowledge of the past. The philologists did not attempt to pick the low hanging epistemic fruits like Ranke, but the culturally most prized fruits, the founding documents of the Western Civilization.

The biblical critics initially divided the Old Testament into documents according to a single simple method, following the assumption that the later editors who collected and homogenized the language of the texts after the Babylonian exile were deterred by an ancient taboo from editing the names of God(s). Therefore, texts that mention different names of God(s) (*Jehovah, El, Elohim, Shaddai*) must have been independent documents originally. Poetic parts of the bible were probably preserved unedited because the editing would have changed the rhyme and meter, and some of these poems also maintain more archaic grammatical forms. Philologists then attempted to infer the genealogies of the constitutive texts and some of the properties of the past they preserved.

Friedrich August Wolf applied in his 1795 *Prolegomena ad Homerum* (1985) the methods of biblical criticism as developed by J. G. Eichhorn for the analysis of the *Iliad* and the *Odyssey*. Wolf concluded that the task of the classical philologist is to infer the histories of texts, the information transmission channels that led to the versions that survived to the present. His task should have been easier than that of biblical critics because there was more evidence about the history of the transmission and editing of Homer than of the bible (Wolf 1985, 173). F. K. Heinrich followed Wolf's model in 1802 to analyze the origins of Hesiod's *Shield of Hercules* (Grafton, Most & Zetzel 1985, 19–26).

"The German historians who applied a critical method to the sources of medieval and early modern history imitated what German classical scholars had already done for the sources of ancient literary and political history" (Grafton 1997, 83–84). Ranke applied the reasoning of the philologists to generate knowledge of history. Despite his denials, Ranke clearly learned how to reason in historiography from Gottfried Hermann who introduced him to the methods of classical philology, which he then imported to historiography (Grafton 1997, 86–93). Before discussing Ranke's contribution to historiographic reasoning further, I should warn the readers that much of what they must have heard and believed about Ranke and his methods is the result of a century-old political campaign of character assassination. Originally, it followed anti-German sentiments among allied historians during the First World War. Ranke, who died aged 90 in 1886 stood accused posthumously of association with German Statism and Imperialism. This accusation conflated Ranke the historian with the much later "Neo-Rankian" school, so-called, that indeed focused on geopolitical history from a Bismarckian blood and soil geopolitical realist ideological perspective. Needless to say, Ranke was not a "neo-Rankean." Arguably, the "paleo-Rankeans" were enlightenment philologists. Ranke used state archives to generate not only political historiography, but also economic, cultural, and intellectual historiography. Ranke even practiced rudimentary semiotics, for example, when he interpreted in his first book the elaborate symbols used in a Renaissance pageant. Ranke was bound by the limits of the evidence he uncovered which generated more political historiography than future historians with access to more diverse types of evidence and better theories to extract information from them would be able to generate. Nevertheless, he did not deny or ignore other branches of historiography or nonpolitical aspects of history. The reduction of his achievements to the much later Bismarckian politics is an anachronistic caricature. This character assassination is exacerbated by the tendency of contemporary critics to use two or three "quotations" of Ranke that are in fact half sentences that create the opposite impression to the meaning of the whole sentence, let alone the whole paragraph in context, to denounce him. As the founder of the generative paradigm in historiography, his methods were replicated and imitated by the very historians who denounced him. Yet, as much as Americans came to convince themselves during the First World War that Hamburgers, Frankfurters, and Berliners (rechristened doughnuts) were American food staples, so did Ranke's methods come to be "domesticated" and disassociated from their origins.

The significance of Ranke's historiography has been neither in his obsolete political values that have no contemporary legacies, nor even in the highly probable historiography he generated from the archives he had access to – later historians would have access to a broader scope of evidence and progress to generate more extensive and detailed historiographies. Ranke's significance was in his ability to *generate* historiographic knowledge reliably, repeatedly, systematically, explicitly, and institutionally in a seminar. Ranke's students learned there to reliably replicate his methods and *generate* historiographic knowledge from evidential inputs that may not individually be reliable enough to transmit knowledge.

The theoretical core of Ranke's generative historiography coincides with that of biblical criticism, classical philology, and comparative linguistics. All these sciences generated knowledge of historical origins from information-preserving coherences between independent evidence by inferring the information chains that connected the historical origin, the source of the information, with the receivers of the information. In Ranke's historiography, the coherences are between primary sources. Ranke recognized that coherences do not have to be of propositional contents. When Ranke encountered propositionally inconsistent documents, for example, reports by the ambassadors of different countries, Ranke did not attempt to evaluate their respective reliabilities and side with the more reliable source, like the best historians who preceded him, like Thucydides. Instead, Ranke discovered their nonpropositional informational coherence to generate new knowledge (Grafton 1997, 52). Ranke examined evidence for links on the information transmission chains that stretch back from the evidential inputs to their common origin.

Ranke became the founder of a new paradigm not just because of the generative methods he received from philology, but because these theories and methods were fruitful in directing him to the discovery of new and surprising evidence and consequently to the generation of new and surprising historiographic knowledge. Ranke's first discovery of evidence was of the Venetian *Relazioni*, three centuries of reports by Venetian ambassadors from European courts. Ranke was the first historian to examine them and then correlate them with independent evidentiary inputs in archives in Rome and Florence. His *German History in the Reformation Era* used the 96 volumes of reports of the Frankfurt deputies at the Imperial Diet 1414–1613. Ranke compared them with independent evidentiary documents in archives in Weimar, Dresden, and Dessau. Ranke found in Brussels the correspondence of Charles V and compared it with independent evidentiary documents in the Paris archives and some of the Italian materials he collected earlier. *The History of Prussia* was based on letters of the French ambassador and independent documents from the Prussian archives. Ranke researched the archives of France, Italy, Belgium, Germany, England, and Spain for his 1853 *History of France*. The discoveries of new evidence allowed Ranke to progressively revise historiography (Gooch 1959, 87–88; Grafton 1997, 52).

Since Ranke, historiography progressed in leaps and bounds by expanding and diversifying the types of evidential inputs that preserve information about the past beyond Ranke's wildest dreams to include material remains and artefacts, the physical environment, art, languages, DNA, and much more. Extracting information from these evidential inputs requires in some cases theories Ranke could not have known about, from carbon 14 dating to genetic analysis to statistical analysis of massive data sets. Yet, historiographic reasoning still consists of the generation of knowledge of history from independent evidential inputs whose coherence is unlikely in the absence of a common origin. In that respect, all historians are Rankeans, inhabiting the paradigm he founded as part of a larger epistemically generative scientific revolution that evolved in continental Europe from the middle of the eighteenth century.

11 Underdetermination: The Limits of Historiographic Reasoning

Parts of history are o*verdetermined*; they generated so much information-preserving evidence that there is more evidence than necessary for inferring their properties. Historians can even afford then to ignore redundant evidence. Unfortunately, the *underdetermination* of historiography by *insufficient* evidence is a more frequent challenge for historiography. Evidence for most of history is scarce. Historiography is at the tender mercy of entropy's arbitrary censorship of the evidence. Though contemporary physics affirms that no information is ever lost in the universe, for example, if a book is burnt, its information is not destroyed, information may be transmuted into practically useless forms that cannot be decoded. Many important and interesting historical events and processes did not generate information signals that reached the present, for example, evidence for the languages and religions of humans during the last ice age, the complete texts of the pre-Socratic philosophers, and the "lost books" of the bible such as the Chronicles of the Kings of Judea and the information they contained about Judean history. Was there a historical Moses, and if so what sort of fellow was he, did he have a farm in Midian, and where was he buried after all? Frustratingly, sometimes the evidence that survives is to trivial aspects of the past. For example, much of what we can know about ancient philosophy was chosen by Diogenes Laertius, a mediocre thinker who had had access to important books that were later lost, but cared little for their philosophical significance, and instead transmitted trivial and unreliable biographic information about the lives of philosophers.

When limited information survived the cruel vicissitudes of time and the censorship of entropy, it may suffice to exclude some hypotheses, but not to discriminate between others. The Neolithic figurines of buxom women that are found all over Europe may be evidence, by analogies from much later cultures, to matriarchal societies if the figurines depict political rulers, or to fertility cults if they are fertility goddesses, or to the sexual taste of Neolithic men if they are Stone-Age pornography.

Underdetermination may also result from the absence of resources to process too much evidence, to infer forests from trees. For example, the degree of complicity of the inhabitants of the occupied lands between Russia and Germany in the Holocaust is fiercely debated. The Soviets attempted to assign responsibility for the Holocaust to Lithuanians and Latvians whose states the USSR destroyed and to West Ukrainians whose national aspirations it crushed, to justify the Soviet occupation. Conversely, Snyder (2015) attempted to shift the exclusive responsibility for the Holocaust to the Germans to minimize the responsibility of local Polish, Ukrainian, Belarusian, and Baltic nationals. When the evidence for local complicity did not support this interpretation, Snyder blamed former collaborators with the Soviet occupation for local complicity in the Holocaust, and disassociated the peasantry, not just from the state and the upper classes such as the Polish Szlachta in societies where class divisions could be extreme, but from the nation itself, proposing that Polish-speaking peasants were not quite Polish. Acknowledging that traditional homegrown anti-Semitism in East Europe, though pervasive, was not genocidal, the question is statistical: To what extent were some East Europeans also responsible for, or complicit in, the Holocaust? How many East Europeans were helpless passive observers and sometimes victims of what Germans did to the Jews, and how many participated in the Holocaust willingly and actively by killing Jews, handing them over to the Germans or to murderous nationalist partisans to be killed, or by refusing to help them? The answer is currently underdetermined, not because there is not enough evidence, but because there is too much of it for any single historian to amalgamate and analyze statistically. More resources and politically impartial research may generate determined answers. Similarly, it is impossible to estimate how many of the people who sheltered Jews did so to denounce and rob them – how many did so for profit that fell short of what they would have gained from getting them killed and robbing them, how many merely were forced to ask the Jews to help cover their own expenses because they were poor, and how many were righteous Christians who risked their lives to save the lives of their compatriots and neighbors. There must have been a continuum with many shades, but the determination of the statistical distribution awaits further research (Tucker 2016).

Underdetermined historiography can be determined by expanding the scope of evidence, by discovering new relevant evidence that can settle old disputes. When a discovery is impossible or unsuccessful, historians may attempt to extract more information from existing evidence by adding information theories or generalizations. These information theories may be based on historical analogies that assume that signals in different contexts convey the same type of information, so decoding theoretical methods are transitive from one context to the next. Analogies and experiments can serve as theoretical "scaffolding" that infers the history of an evidential input as if it were another analogous type of trace (Currie 2018). The promise of comparative historiography has been to determine hitherto underdetermined historiographic hypotheses and disputes by using analogous evidence to support information theories that can extract new information from old evidence. For example, the decisive proof for Wolf's hypotheses about the oral traditional origins of the Homeric sagas came from evidence about comparable illiterate bards in Yugoslavia (Parry 1971). The information nested in archaeological discoveries of structures or artefacts of unknown function may be decoded by comparison with analogous artefacts or structures used today or in the recent past. Information theories and generalizations that extract more information from known evidence can also have an experimental basis, especially when extracting information from material remains and artefacts. Archaeologists experiment with replicas of ancient tools and simulate construction methods. Computerized modeling of complex processes can generate surprising results (Currie 2018). Such experiments are also useful for the elimination of underdetermined hypotheses by determining how history could not have been, what techniques would not have produced the evidence.

Faced with evidential underdetermination, historians may revise their hypotheses to make them less informative, reduce their detail or "Granularity" (Malaterre 2024). Other historians may seek the trickier assistance of social science theories that are about types rather than tokens. The historiographic tokens, however, are not identical with their social theoretical types. History is almost always more complex and multivariate than the theories. The fitting of theories and types to historical tokens in complex contexts requires interpretations of the social scientific theories that are ad hoc and consequently, underdetermined – a theory must have more than one instantiation to be tested. Different ad hoc interpretations of the same social science theory can be mutually inconsistent. The ad hoc interpretations are more accurate than the theories that inspired them, but they have a narrower, underdetermining evidentiary justifications.

The social manifestation of underdetermined historiography is the absence of the kind of expert consensus that is manifest in determined parts of historiography. Applied social science theories and their mutually inconsistent interpretations are manifested in schools, united by social science theories that are then further fragmented according to increasingly precise ad hoc interpretations to fit accurately a limited evidentiary base. Following the inconsistencies between the ad hoc theoretical interpretations, evidentiary justifications of ad hoc hypotheses are not transitive to each other; nor can they be *deduced* from the

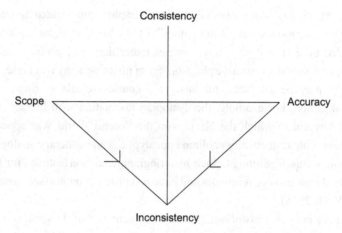

Figure 2 The fitting of social science theories and types to historical token.

social science theories they interpret because they must be interpreted inconsistently to fit the evidence. The following diagram models the dilemma that
historiographic attempts to interpret social science theories to determine underdetermined historiography must face. Historiography can try to use a well-
corroborated social science theory of broad scope, but the theory would not be
sufficiently accurate to fit the evidence; it can interpret the theory to fit the
evidence, but then it would lose the evidential scope that corroborated the
theory; or it can try to maintain scope and accuracy by developing multiple
inconsistent ad hoc interpretations of the same theory, which seems to be the
choice most historians who borrow from the social sciences make (see
Figure 2).

No matter which point on the preceding triangle is chosen, the aggregated
cognitive value of the choice remains low in comparison with both scientific
theories and determined historiography, as long as the evidence remains constant and insufficient.

12 Counterfactual Historiographic Reasoning

It is debatable whether historiographic counterfactuals can be justified by
reasoning, and if so, whether this reasoning resembles historiographic "factual"
reasoning simpliciter. The outputs of historiographic counterfactual reasoning
would, by definition, differ from the outputs of historiographic reasoning
because they outline the properties of events that never happened, whereas
the outputs of historiographic reasoning are properties of events that probably
did happen. The processes of reasoning may also have different inputs, use
different evidence.

Some, mostly historians, claim that historiographic counterfactuals are literary fiction or are mostly just "parlor games" (Evans 2016). If so, their evaluation is founded on aesthetic or political values rather than on reasoning, and the aesthetic or politically reductive philosophies of historiography that I rejected in Section 4 may be as useful for analyzing counterfactuals as they are for historical fiction. For example, the dystopian fascination with literary depictions of a world in which the Nazis won the Second World War appeals to fascination with aesthetically sublime apocalyptic scenes, literary analogies to Hieronymus Busch paintings. Such historiographic counterfactuals, for better or worse, do not involve reasoning and have no epistemic inputs (see Rosenfeld 2016, Woolf 2016).

But there are other historiographic counterfactuals that do seem to follow reasoning from evidence, for example, counterfactuals about historical succession: Had Donald Trump been relieved of his presidency before January of 2020, Mike Pence would have become the 46th president of the United States. Had Lee Harvey Oswald missed J. F. Kennedy, L. B. Johnson would not have succeeded him then as the President of the United States. These are highly probable, determined, counterfactuals. Other counterfactuals are underdetermined. For example, how different would US policies have been in relation to what they actually were had Kennedy continued to serve or had Trump been replaced by Pence? The evaluation of such counterfactuals as, for example, whether the Vietnam War and the civil rights policies of the Johnson administration would have been different under a continued Kennedy administration, are less determined than succession counterfactuals, but are still far from epistemically arbitrary because historiographic evidence may be used to infer such historiographic counterfactual knowledge, in the preceding cases, evidence for the contemporary constraints on any American administration, statements by Kennedy and Pence about their views and intentions or testimonies left by others about their intentions and wishes.

At the opposite end to the "parlor game" denial of counterfactual reasoning, it may be argued, following David Lewis' (1973) counterfactual theory of causation, that counterfactual reasoning is indistinguishable from some historiographic reasoning because whenever historians make causal claims and justify them, they assume, at least implicitly, a historiographic counterfactual: Had the cause not occurred, nor would have the effect. The evaluation of counterfactuals, according to David Lewis' theory, is derived from historiographic factual reasoning because historiographic counterfactuals are justified by measuring their resemblance to factual historiography: The counterfactual most similar to factual historiography is the most plausible. This further entangles factual with counterfactual historiography because factual causal propositions depend on

counterfactual propositions, and the evaluation or justification of the counterfactuals is based on factual historiographic reasoning that infers what probably
happened in history (Maar 2016, Ben-Menahem 2016, Sunstein 2016, Nolan
2016). How to measure similarity between factual and counterfactual historiography, and how similar is similar enough, remain vague in counterfactual
theories of causation; indeed, this has led to academic jokes, for example
(with thanks to my friends at UC Berkeley for sharing): The impoverished
adjunct professor of ethics chats with the impoverished adjunct professor of
logic and exclaims: "The world is so unfair! Had I been Alex Soros (the
historian son of billionaire George Soros) I would have been wealthier than
he is!" The logician retorts: "This is nonsense, had you been Alex Soros you
would have been exactly as wealthy as he is." The ethics adjunct remains
unconvinced: "You want to tell me that had I been Alex Soros, I would not
have been able still to get to teach Business Ethics somewhere?!"

But the counterfactual theory of historiographic causation is neither sufficient, nor necessary, nor clear enough to account for historiographic causation.
Counterfactual theories of historiographic causation (Lewis 1973, 1986) are
challenged by *omissions, preventers, delayers, hasteners, transitivity, overdetermination*, and *preemption*: Omissions are problematic for counterfactual
theories of causation because historiographic texts consider omissions causes,
for example the *omission* of action by France and Britain when Germany
occupied the Rhineland is one of the *causes* of the Second World War, which
Germany lost because it *did not have* the atomic bomb. Causal counterfactuals,
by contrast, do not consider omissions causes (Lewis 2004, 99–104; Hall
2004b; Maar 2016). *Causal transitivity* has counterintuitive results for counterfactual theories of causation, for example, Nazism caused the Second World
War. The Second World War caused the defeat of Germany. The defeat of
Germany caused the founding of NATO, *ergo* Nazism caused transitively the
founding of NATO. Some defenders of counterfactual theories of causation bit
the counterintuitive bullet to accept transitive causation. Others disaggregated
the concept of cause to develop a pluralistic account, allowing one type of cause
to be transitive (Lewis 2004, 93–99; Hall 2004a, 2004b). Factors that "*prevent*,"
"*delay*," and "*hasten*" effects of other causes appear counterintuitively to satisfy
causal counterfactual criteria (see Hall 2004a & b).

Overdetermining causes and *preempting* causes do not satisfy counterfactual
conditions. For example, since Julius Caesar's death on the Ides of March was
overdetermined by twenty-three assassins, individual assassins cannot satisfy
counterfactual causal conditions. The assassination attempt against Israel's
ambassador to London, Shlomo Argov, in 1982 preempted other causes that
Israeli Defense Minister Ariel Sharon would have used as *causa belli* for

invading Lebanon according to the previously planned "Oranim Plan," in the false expectation of deciding its civil war with a Christian-Maronite victory and pro-Israeli government, so the assassination attempt cannot satisfy the counterfactual causal dependency condition. Philosophers proposed elaborate methods to overcome, or at least bypass, such challenges (Collins 2004; Hall 2004a & 2004b; Schaffer 2004) such as describing effects as "fine-grained" or "fragile" to avoid causal overdetermination and preemption (Lewis 1986, 2004, 85–88; Coady 2004; Maar 2016). But the conceptualization of effects as "fragile" is challenging, especially when effects like victory or defeat in war, liberalism or totalitarianism, like pregnancy, allow only binary values that cannot be finegrained or fragile to preempt preemption or determine overdetermination. Lewis' characterization of fragility is vague, partly because he wanted to avoid deciding whether the counterfactual event is a version of, or a variation on, the factual one, or just different. A counterfactual account of historiographic causation then is insufficient unless the theory becomes very complex and uses ad hoc remedies to avoid patent absurdities.

A counterfactual theory of historiographic causation is unnecessary because knowledge of historical causal chains can be the epistemic output of evidential inputs and historiographic reasoning like other aspects of historiography. Counterfactual accounts of historiographic causation are redundant because historical causal sequences can send information signals about their properties to the evidence. The evidence can transmit or generate knowledge of the historical causal sequences. For example, if a leader confided to a private diary information about intentions, reasons, and plans for action, the diary preserves the information about the historical causal link between intention and action. If the leader repeated these reasons and plans in personal correspondence and in conversation with aids and confidants who recorded it, then it is possible to further generate this causal knowledge. Counterfactuals, just like covering regularities, rational choice models, and emphatic understanding, can support historiographic causal assertions, but are not necessary if there is sufficient evidence.

If at least some historiographic counterfactuals are neither fiction nor logically equivalent to historiographic causation, there is counterfactual historiographic reasoning and it must consider counterfactuals as functional outputs of evidential inputs. The inputs to historiographic counterfactuals must both subtract from, and add to, the evidence that factual historiography uses as inputs. Historiographic counterfactuals must presume by *fiat* counterfactual evidence that determines the antecedents of counterfactuals. We may call this evidence "ghostly" because it is not specified but must be presumed to infer that, for example, Germany won the war, or that J. F. Kennedy was not assassinated, or that Trump did not complete his term of office. The ghostly evidence must be consistent with the rest of the evidential inputs for historiographic counterfactuals. Part of the actual historiographic evidence necessarily, by definition, must contradict the ghostly evidence and disprove the historiographic counterfactuals to make it into a counterfactual; for example, there is plenty of reliable evidence that Germany lost the war, J. F. Kennedy was assassinated and succeeded by L. B. Johnson, and Trump not only completed his term of office, but even sought to extend it further. So, for the historiographic evidence to fit the "ghostly" evidence, the evidence against the counterfactual antecedent must be *truncated*; we agree tacitly to suspend belief in parts of the evidence. We tacitly agree for the purpose of considering a counterfactual about Nazi victory in the war, to "not mention the (actual) war" (in a nod to *Fawlty Towers*), evidence for how the war actually ended. The complete counterfactual then is a function of the consistent truncated and ghostly evidence.

Historiographic counterfactual reasoning depends on whether there is sufficient evidence, following the truncation of evidence that contradicts ghostly counterfactual evidence, to infer the consequents of the counterfactual. This depends both on how much historiographic evidence is there to begin with, and on how much of it must be truncated to avoid incoherence with the "ghostly" counterfactual evidence. For example, to determine a counterfactual on what would have happened had Nazi Germany won the Second World War, it is not enough to just assume ghostly evidence to German victory; the rest of the evidence has to be consistent with it through truncation, which in this case, as in other historiographic counterfactuals that presume major changes in world history, is massive. The whole evidence for European history and global geopolitics would have to be truncated to avoid internally contradictory incoherent evidence (see Elster 1978). When so much of the evidence is truncated, there is not much left in evidential inputs to infer the consequent of the counterfactual antecedent from the evidence. The counterfactual becomes then fantasy fiction, which can still be interesting in many respects, with a nod to Philip K. Dick, but evidential determination would not be one of its virtues.

Still, more minor historiographic counterfactual changes to history may not require such an invasive truncation of evidence that would not leave enough of it for reasoning. For example, evidence for the death or survival of any individual may be truncated while leaving quite a lot of evidence about their historical context unaffected. In the easy cases of counterfactual succession, the evidence for laws or norms of succession and the degree of respect for them in a historical period are not truncated by ghostly evidence about death or abdication, or conversely survival, and that evidence suffices to generate with high reliability the counterfactual consequents. In more complex cases, for example, a counterfactual in which Hitler dies in the First World War or successfully commits suicide after the failure of his Beer Hall Putsch, still much of the evidence survives truncation; the evidence for what happened in Germany during and in the aftermath of the War does not contradict the ghostly evidence for Hitler's death. Of the remaining evidence, documents about the organizations and personalities of the extreme right during the Weimar Republic and the weaknesses of the Republic may suffice to infer who or what kind of leaders would have vowed for power in the absence of Hitler, and how different their counterfactual policies would have been from Hitler's. For example, though Hitler was hardly the only anti-Semitic politician in Germany, he was evidently the only one to be entirely obsessed with Jews above all other issues including winning the war. Many historians of the Holocaust agree with Milton Himmelfarb's (1984) famous counterfactual formulation: "No Hitler, No Holocaust." Hitler was a necessary condition for the Holocaust. Without him, Germany could have still been a belligerent, authoritarian if not totalitarian, state, but the Jews would not have been targeted for extermination.

Apart from the addition of "ghostly evidence" and the truncation of actual evidence that contradicts it, counterfactual historiographic reasoning is quite similar to factual historiographic reasoning. When there is sufficient evidence left after the truncation, counterfactuals can have high degrees of posterior probability. When historiographic evidence is poor even before the truncation, or if it is severely truncated to be consistent with the ghostly evidence, the resulting counterfactuals may be vastly underdetermined because many epistemic outputs may be consistent with the evidence. Some counterfactuals, for example assuming the Roman Empire developed the atom bomb or Leonardo Da Vinci flew to the moon, truncate practically all the evidence and leave nothing for any reasoning, so the counterfactual becomes pure fiction that may be judged only on its aesthetic-literary merits like novels in the alternative history fantasy genre.

Though determined historiographic counterfactuals are not necessary for the inference of causal relations in historiography, they are necessary for evaluating whether historical events were necessary or contingent, because estimates of historical necessity and contingency require evaluation of the sensitivity of events to initial conditions, which requires the inference of counterfactuals: Had the cause not taken place, would something similar to the actual effect still have happened, in which case it was necessary, or nothing like the actual effect would have happened, in which case the effect was contingent on the cause. For example, the frequent references in historiography to "triggering causes" or metaphorically to "the match that lit the fire" imply that the effect of the triggering event or something very similar to it would have happened sooner or later anyway. As mentioned above, the assassination attempt against Ambassador Argov in London in 1982 triggered the Israeli invasion of Lebanon, but the Oranim Plan would have been executed anyway with some other trigger to a similar effect. Necessary processes are insensitive to initial conditions, often because they are overdetermined, when multiple redundant causes lead to the same effect (Ben-Menahem 1997, 2009, 2016; Tucker 2004, 226–239). Processes that would have turned entirely different had things been slightly different, like the proverbial "for want of a nail, the kingdom fell," are contingent. For example, "no Hitler, no Holocaust" means that the Holocaust was contingent on Hitler. Had Hitler not been the leader of Germany, no other leader would have initiated something similar, and millions of people would have survived. In other cases, the evidence may not be as decisive. For example, had Gavrilo Princip missed the Archduke, would there have still been a First World War because the system of alliances in Europe destabilized geopolitics or because German imperial ambitions could not have been satisfied without a war?

The categorization of factual or counterfactual consequents as contingent or necessary depends also on how detailed, or information rich, they are. *Ceteris paribus,* the more detailed and precise they are, the more contingent, and vice versa. Kim Sterelny (2016) described the degree of precision of consequents as between the "robust" and the "fragile." "Historical trajectories are robust when they depend only on aggregate effects of interactions in populations. For then historical trajectories are screened off from idiosyncratic individual decisions, improbable local outcomes, and outcomes that depend on tiny quirks of specific circumstances. The outcome is not counterfactually sensitive to such small variations in initial conditions and ongoing context" (Sterelny 2016, 532 cf. Inkpen & Turner 2012; compare Tucker 2009).

Ceteris paribus, the more complex is the counterfactual, the more factors and causal links must be considered and the more difficult it is to find sufficient evidence to determine it. Therefore, the most determined judgments of contingency and necessity deal with a single consequent effect rather than stretch the process across several causal links that become more complex and involve the interactions of many factors that require truncating more and more of the evidence to generate more and more evidentially demanding counterfactuals. This evidentially self-reinforcing vicious circle of less evidence for more information-rich counterfactual hypotheses collapses fairly quickly into speculative fiction (see Evans 2016).

13 Historiographic Reasoning in Contexts

The judgment whether a historiographic posterior probability is sufficiently probable to be considered knowledge depends not only on the evidence but also on historiographic context, on pragmatic considerations. As *Epistemic Contextualism* suggests, the effect of knowledge on practical interests determines the probabilistic threshold for knowledge (DeRose 2009). This is evident in common law, where there are different standards of evidence for criminal law (beyond reasonable doubt), civil law (the preponderance of evidence), and in licensing cases (presumption of guilt: Next time a traffic policeman asks you for your driver's license, try asking him if he can prove you do not have one beyond reasonable doubt?!) that correlate with the potential severity of the consequences for the accused. In most historiographic cases, the standard of proof is comparable to that in civil cases, following the preponderance of evidence. But when the present effects of historiography are significant, the probabilistic threshold for historiographic knowledge may rise to "beyond reasonable doubt." For example, historians may infer from a police document that somebody was a spy for the secret police of the Habsburg monarchy in the nineteenth century. The same kind of evidence with the same reliability may not suffice for concluding beyond reasonable doubt that a living person was an informer for the Communist secret police in the same place. Consequently, as the context of historiography moves with history to the future, historiographic outputs that were considered insufficiently justified to be considered knowledge may become sufficiently justified, not because they become more probable, but because their contexts change and cease to matter for the living; as Steve Allen put it, (historical) comedy is tragedy plus time.

Occasionally, however, the historiographic bar for knowledge may, conversely, rise, when historical events that were hitherto considered insignificant for the living become significant parts of a narrative, especially because of new political uses of historiography. For example, nationalism is usually accompanied by the construction of a nationalist historiographic narrative that often stakes claims for territories on the alleged basis of historical collective property rights. The claims about history then involve historiography in debates over who was where first and who stole what from whom when. As a moral claim the whole historiographic discourse of who came first may appear ridiculous, because obviously except for the Americas, Homo erectus or Neanderthals were there first. The Roman Empire preceded the invasion of the Germanic, Slavic, and Finno-Ugric tribes into Europe, and the Basques may have been first in Europe, so the same logic would recommend that the Germans, Slavs, Hungarians, and Finns should return to Asia and let Vatican City take over Europe, before ceding it to the Basques who would then transfer it to the descendants of the Neanderthals, which according to recent genetic evidence means all non-African humans, so nothing needs to change much except that Europeans and Asians need to learn to respect their Neanderthal ancestors and stop ridiculing them. Be that as it may, once nationalist political claims attempt to ground themselves in history, it becomes important to ascertain those historiographic claims, and the bar for proof is raised, for example, it may be pointed out that many of the "holy graves" Israeli Jews and Palestinian Moslems fight over in the holy land were miraculously revealed to the Christian Byzantine Flavia Julia Helena, the mother of Emperor Constantine the Great, who would become Saint Helena in her pilgrimage in the early fourth century. Needless to point out, Saint Helena had no training in biblical archaeology and she identified sites that had been abandoned for centuries without evidence beyond the guidance of the Holy Spirit.

Still, these pragmatic contextual influences do not affect the probability of the historiographic outputs themselves that are exclusively the functional products of their evidential inputs. Pragmatic contexts affect only which posterior probabilities are considered high enough to satisfy the requirements for *knowledge*. Changes in epistemic contexts cannot transmit, generate, or decay grounds for knowledge. When changes in epistemic contexts raise or lower thresholds for knowledge, without changes in the evidence or reasoning, knowledge is neither generated nor decays. A better way to express the "appearance" or "disappearance" of knowledge that results from contextual changes may be to say that knowledge is *manifested* or is *concealed* by its context, to emphasize the absence of generative or decaying epistemic processes. The manifestation or concealment of knowledge as a result of changes in epistemic contexts resemble athletic triumphs or defeats that do not result from the athlete running faster or slower, but from moving the finishing line backward or forward.

14 Invalid and False Historiographic Reasoning

The analysis of historiographic reasoning that I presented is useful not just for understanding how evidential inputs transmit and generate historiographic knowledge, but also for analyzing what happens when historiographic reasoning goes awry, for example, if it ignores reliable evidence, accepts transmissions of unreliable evidence, or treats dependent evidence as if it were independent. Invalid and false historiographic reasonings are the dark mirror image of the historiographic reasoning we analyzed.

Some false or invalid historiographic reasoning is unintentionally erroneous. Others argue backwards, from pre-established conclusions and use false evidence or invalid forms of reasoning from the evidence to rhetorically support these conclusions. For example, if the conclusion must be the ancient and heroic origins of the nation, somebody will manufacture false heroic sagas to back up the claim, for example, the poems of Ossian and his many imitators in Europe. If the conclusion is that patriarchal Christianity suppressed the original female element in the religion, some German Egyptologist in Florida with an interesting career choice will manufacture a gospel about Jesus' wife (Sabar 2020). The types of pre-established conclusions behind mistakes in historiographic reasoning do not matter for identifying and criticizing the mistakes because the mistakes are in reasoning and not necessarily in politics – one may believe in equal rights to all genders without presuming that Jesus must have had a wife. Politics is entirely irrelevant for and distinct from historiographic reasoning, the epistemology of knowledge of history.

Historians may use probable historiographic outputs for political purposes, for example, to learn from past mistakes and successes. Historiography is relevant for human affairs and can be applied to help solve political problems, or at least advise on how to prevent making them worse. Without historical experience, as Santayana (1954) observed, societies are doomed to eternal childhood, without experience, they must repeat historical mistakes. "Those who cannot remember the past are condemned to repeat it," as he famously put it in his 1905 book. Santayana argued that historical progress results from learning from history through historiography. Societies devoid of knowledge of history are condemned to repeating cyclically the same mistakes every two generations, when personal memories fade and disappear, which may well explain the current popularity of the political plans that failed miserably in the second third of the twentieth century, but are not remembered by the living. Maintaining historical lessons across the generations can prevent the eternal recurrence of history in bigenerational cycles. Historiography plants signposts that warn novice historical drivers not to enter historical cul-de-sacs that lead to cliff tops and abysses. But to achieve this political goal, the probable historiographic truth must come first and not be influenced by political considerations.

For political considerations to trump historiographic reason, the politics is often of the passions, powerful enough to overwhelm reason. The political passions result in "emotivist historiography," when under the influence of the passions beliefs about history become influenced by narrative expressions of passions and emotions rather than probable outputs of reliable epistemic inputs and reasoning. For example, hate or fear, the most powerful passions, are expressed in narratives where the objects of hate or fear committed atrocities and damned be any evidence to the contrary. The absence of evidence can similarly be ignored. The previous Bayesian analysis of historiographic reasoning is useful for analyzing types of such historiographic fallacies.

Confirmation bias leads historians to look for, and consider only evidence that supports their pre-established beliefs. Psychological-behavioral explanations of failures to diligently search for and consider new evidence, to update historiographic posterior probabilities and consequently prior probabilities for the next historiographic inference, include the "bandwagon effect" when historians fear having different opinions than their perceived peer group; and *anchoring* – the failure to adjust posterior probabilities of hypotheses following new evidence due to inability to give up on cherished beliefs. Extreme forms of confirmation bias happen when passions take over reason entirely and the evidence cannot refute or revise historiographic narratives that express the passions in narrative form because evidence has no bearing on the passions. For example, Holocaust deniers and supporters of terrorism usually cannot bear the thought that their favorite movements, organizations, and states committed heinous crimes. So they ignore or dismiss as unreliable the vast independent and reliable evidence for the atrocities. Fear and hate may cause narratives about immigrants in North America committing more crimes than natives, though there is overwhelming rigorous statistical evidence to the contrary. But this evidence does not correspond with expressions of the passions for scapegoating immigrants in North America, so it is ignored.

The wholesale denial of the evidence is rare in institutional or professional historiography, and is easily recognized. But it is easier to overlook selective use of evidence that truncates only a part of it, as in counterfactuals, to produce distorted historiography. For example, some neo-totalitarian apologists who want to "normalize" Nazism and Communism as unexceptional in the context of modern history, do not deny the Holocaust or the gulags, but note, correctly, that most subjects of totalitarian states were neither direct perpetrators nor immediate victims. Since the large majority of Germans were neither Jews nor opposition leaders nor members of the SS and agents of the Gestapo, arguably the "everyday" experience of Nazism was of full employment, Wagner, and *autobahns* and later the occasional sojourn into Poland. Similarly, since most East Europeans were neither agents of the Communist secret police nor persecuted dissidents, Communism was allegedly experienced by most initially as industrialization and later as piecemeal advances in the standard of living, consumerism, and pop culture punctuated by the occasional May Day manifestations and occasional Soviet-friendly assistance, most notably, invasions. The partial use of evidence constructs the totalitarian everyday as a variety of modernity, comparable to nontotalitarian contemporary modern democracies. The neo-totalitarian historians deliberately ignore the evidence

for state terrorism and vast and broad fear in society, monolithic social stratifi-
cation, and absence of civil society that distinguish totalitarian from democratic
modernization. State terrorism is not committed just to eliminate real and
imagined opponents or punish enemies, the immediate victims. The terror is
designed to control through fear atomized subjects who remain embedded in
"everyday life." For this reason, the atrocities that totalitarian regimes commit
can never be entirely secret. The general population must know enough about
them to be scared, and that fear must permeate every social interaction to
prevent the spontaneous emergence of civil society. Atomized individuals
must fear not just the state, but each other because they cannot know who is
a friend, who is a foe, and who is the informer. Totalitarianism deniers must
ignore the evidence for how totalitarian regimes forced ordinary people to
become complicit in their own oppression to generate whitewashed representations of totalitarianism. The evidence for the terror that permeates society is
both direct and indirect, but requires looking for. If it is ignored, it results in
a counterfactual historiography masquerading as factual.

The historiographic research program about the "history of the everyday"
how ordinary people lived and perceived their environment in history, irrespective of high politics, is useful for understanding periods when there is evidence
that everyday life embedded in civil society was relatively unaffected, independent, of politics and political change; for example in France after the radical
revolutionary changes brought about by the Revolution and the Napoleonic
wars, for much of the nineteenth century, the period for which this historiographic approach was introduced originally. It is possible to study the world of
"Madame Bovary" without considering evidence for political upheavals in
Paris that had little or no effect on civil society, economic development, and
life in general in the provinces once feudalism ended, the land was redistributed,
and the wars of the Napoleonic era concluded. But it is impossible to study
everyday life during totalitarianism or during periods of mass warfare without
inferring information from evidence for political violence and terror emanating
from the political center since they radically affected the everyday lives of most
ordinary people in the absence of civil society and following the state domin-
ation of the economy. Neo-totalitarian microstudies deliberately ignore evidence that frames events in small places in their larger historical context.
General conclusions about periods and localities require comparative analysis
with other localities to find what is common and what is distinct. If historians
ignore comparative evidence, and evidence for how the totalitarian macro-level
was reflected on the micro-level, decontextualized microhistoriography creates
the false impression of historical continuity and "normalcy" on the local level.

The opposite mistake to ignoring relevant evidence is *the acceptance of unreliable evidence* as if it was an information-preserving reliable input. For example, *anachronism* is the indiscriminate use of the present as evidence for the past, without distinguishing present evidence that preserves historical information from recent properties of the present that do not preserve information from deeper history. *Literalism* is a type of anachronism that does not consider that language, the meanings and references of words, evolve and mutate historically. Literalism assumes erroneously that current uses of language and conceptual frameworks preserve reliably historical meanings and conceptual frameworks and reads historical texts or translated texts from other languages as if they were written in contemporary languages (Tucker 2006).

Wrong inferences about channels of historical information transmission from historical events to evidence may lead to the evaluation of unreliable evidence as preserving information reliably from historical events. For example, Niebuhr, a precursor of Ranke, considered evidential sources for early Roman history that were written centuries later reliable by speculatively hypothesizing channels of information transmission, *carmina* banquet songs, funeral panegyrics, and annals kept by high priests, for which there was insufficient evidence (Momigliano 1977, 235–236). Consequently, Niebuhr's historiography of early Rome projected later Roman realities on earlier periods. Similarly, in his youth Nietzsche invented baroque speculative genealogies for literary texts with little or no supporting evidence. Nietzsche attempted to infer a Germanic origin myth about the Eastern Goth king Ermanarich by proposing elaborate speculative genealogies about secondary sources that were considerably later than the events they described. Nietzsche further attempted to infer from received versions of the Greek poet Theognis their original constitutive documents by inventing speculative histories of transmissions, additions, reductions, and editions of the texts, all without evidence (Jensen 2013, 7–56). Boy to man, Nietzsche continued to invent genealogies with little or no evidence. The mature Nietzsche considered aspects of the present that did not preserve historical information as reliable receivers of information from the deep past. Most famously, he claimed that Judeo-Christian morality preserves information about ancient slave-priests outwitting noble heroes by inventing morality. Some other "genealogical" interpretations of history from Nietzsche through Foucault to Assman similarly invent historical genealogies where allegedly information was transmitted to the present without any evidence. These baseless genealogies are narrative expressions of the passion to discredit aspects of the present as receivers and preservers of historical tainted traditions, thereby "exposing" their ignoble alleged origins. The political targets of these authors differed. Nietzsche and Assman targeted Judaism and by implication Christianity. Foucault was more interested in discrediting liberalism and the enlightenment (Wolin 2013; Tucker 2020). But again, the politics are insignificant because the evidence does not support the genealogical claims for information transmission.

Edward Burnett Tylor initiated cultural anthropology in an attempt to trace cultural information transmission from past to present. He introduced the concept of *"survivals* by habit rather than by function," as cultural equivalents to Darwin's *rudiments* – biological homologies, information-preserving traits in the present that retain reliably information from the deep past because the traits do not convey particular evolutionary advantage or disadvantage. Mandelbaum (1977, 97–103) criticized Tylor and another founder of Anthropology, John Lubbock, for failing to distinguish cultural coherences that preserve information from a common origin, from functional similarities that resulted from convergent evolution, like the independent inventions of agriculture, seafaring, and domestications of animals; or in biology, wings and eyes. Mandelbaum criticized, for example, the baseless tracing of the modern habit of wearing earrings to the ancient habit of sticking bones in noses.

The Indo-European philological hypothesis and subsequent philological discoveries were paradigmatically successful applications of historiographic reasoning at the turn of the nineteenth century. The inference of the common origin of the Indo-European languages has been founded on linguistic information theories that distinguished reliable, information-preserving, parts of language (grammatical structure, names of places, fauna and flora, body parts, immediate family members) from those that mutate too frequently to preserve information (e.g. words of politeness and trade). The overwhelming correlations between reliable, information-preserving, parts of the Indo-European languages implied probable common origins. But the philological evidence does not preserve information about the historical existence of an *Urvolk* that spoke the *Ursprache* in *Urheimat* and shared *Urmythen*. Much of the Indo-European branch of anthropology has been founded on this false reasoning apparently to serve ethnic or racist mythologies (Lincoln 1999).

Failure to consider prior probabilities, in addition to the reliabilities of evidential inputs, can lead to overestimation of posterior probabilities of information transmitted from reliable sources who make outlandish claims. When the prior probability of *transmitted* information from a single origin is low, the probability of the historiographic output decreases. By contrast, when knowledge is *generated* from multiple coherent and independent evidential inputs, low prior probabilities can increase the posterior probability of outputs because it is unlikely that they would cohere randomly on something unlikely and surprising without some common origin. Highly informative, very detailed, multiple, coherent, and independent evidentiary inputs can generate knowledge far more probable than the reliabilities of the independent inputs that may have too low posterior probabilities to transmit knowledge. *Psychologically but not logically* this leads to a common *fallacious association* between high posterior probability and low prior probability of information-rich hypotheses *transmitted rather than generated by a single source*. Single testimonial sources that attempt to deceive, or disinform may attempt to exploit this psychological association by transmitting detailed and elaborate confabulations. This psychological association was used by forgers of historiographic texts (Grafton 1990) and is used by internet scammers today, who tell elaborate highly detailed stories, for example about fortunes deposited in banks by deceased dictators, though the reliability of a testimony is not affected by its degree of detail, which may reflect the creative imagination of the witness. The posterior probability of *transmitted* testimonial information *decreases rather than increases* the more improbable is the information. But even intelligence analysts who should understand this deception technique can fall for this scheme when encountering an articulate single source blessed by rich and vivid imagination with attention for imaginary details who tells them what they want to hear. Most spectacularly, Rafid Ahmed Alwan al-Janabi, alias "Curveball," an Iraqi defector to Germany supplied German Intelligence (BND) fantastically detailed information that therefore had low prior probability about Iraq's chemical weapons of mass destruction program in mobile vehicles and bird seed factories. The posterior probability of what a single, uncorroborated, source testifies to decreases when the prior probabilities of the transmitted information are detailed, of lower prior probability. Had there been another coherent but independent testimony to the same effect, the posterior probability would have indeed quantum leaped. But there was no other independent testimony for the chemical WMD fantasies because there were no WMD factories and deposits left in Iraq. Still, American and German security services fell for these stories partly because they were so elaborate, like marks who believe emails with elaborate stories about bank deposits of deposed Nigerian or Libyan dictators that require just a small upfront payment to unlock plundered riches (Tucker 2023).

The coherence or incoherence of independent units of evidence do not affect their individual reliabilities. It is a mistake to increase the assessment of the reliabilities of units of evidence because they cohere, or decrease it because they do not cohere. The reliabilities of evidential inputs are assessed prior to the process of reasoning that transmits or generates historiographic knowledge. The coherence of multiple, independent, evidential inputs affects positively only the posterior probability of the historiographic outputs they generate through historiographic reasoning. Forgers use this fallacy to produce multiple, mutually dependent sources, such as rumors that corroborate each other's stories to generate an invalid inference of reliability from coherence.

Independent coherent evidence can generate knowledge, but historians may *mistake dependent evidence that cannot generate but at most transmit knowledge for independent evidence.* This is one of the main perils of basing historiography on oral testimonies collected after the events; the other is their low reliability because of the unreliability of memory which as just noted, can be invalidly inferred as high from the coherence between the testimonies, though coherence cannot infer reliability. Testimonies are dependent if the witnesses communicated with each other about the historical events or received information from another common information source such as movies or books about the events they testify about. Rather than being able to generate knowledge, such evidence at most retransmits information from a single source on which the others depend.

The most extreme type of information transmission under the guise of generation is from *rumors*. Rumors retransmit unreliably numerous times information from *an unknown source* who may have been unreliable or deliberately deceptive. Reasoning from historical rumors as if they were independent testimonies generates false outputs. This is particularly obvious when the reported rumors are old and reflect in narrative form strong emotion. For example, though the Nazis committed genocide and murdered and tortured and inflicted horrendous suffering on millions of innocent and vulnerable people, they did not turn their victims' corpses into bars of soap after they gassed them. That was a rumor that may have been started by a malicious Nazi terrorist, but was spread by terrorized victims who put in narrative form their feelings of terror and dread. Similarly, rumors about sadomasochist sexual exploitation during the Holocaust of the kind an author and survivor popularized and commercialized under the pseudonym Ka-Tsetnik in his fictional "Stalag genre" novels cannot transmit or generate knowledge. Recently, a German court was forced to intervene when a historian based a published account of an exploitative sexual relations in a concentration camp between a dominating German guard and a dominated Jewish inmate on half-a-century-old rumors which the survivor denied, pronouncing the work as founded on "research misconduct" and "insufficient evidence" (Batty 2020; Morgan 2021). Then, passionate political polarization and social media herd mentality took over the case to suppress reason, as the perpetrator of research misconduct attempted to present herself as a victim and this evidentially baseless tormenting of a Holocaust victim and her family as a case of free speech thwarted by a conservative court, and raised money from "supporters" to pay the symbolic fine the court imposed. Yet, it is a category mistake to consider historiography that is founded on rumors that knowingly attempt to humiliate a survivor and her family, a case of free speech rather than ill-willed fallacious reasoning.

Ignoring auxiliary evidence for the context of the evidence may lead to *misinterpretations* considering *the absence of evidence as evidence for absence.* For example, totalitarian societies generate fewer politically candid diaries and personal correspondence, opinion polls, and voting records, than liberal societies. Direct and explicit contemporary evidence for fear, humiliation, self-alienation, collaboration, resentment, and resistance is underwhelming because victims of totalitarian regimes prudently did not generate evidence that could have been used against them or their friends. Historians who attempt to apologize for totalitarianism or even deny that it ever existed "infer" from the paucity of such evidence that people were not terrorized, humiliated, and so on. Similarly they infer from the paucity of evidence for popular knowledge of atrocities that the true nature of the regime was unknown to many of its supporters, who supported "sanitized" versions of Nazism and Communism because they did not know where their "Jewish" or "bourgeois" neighbors were taken.

In other contexts, absence of evidence is indeed evidence for absence. For example, archaeological digs of the sites of villages where the ancestral Israelite population lived *before* biblical times discovered hundreds of years of buried bones of domestic animals. But no pig bones were discovered. In this context, the absence of evidence for consumption of pork is evidence for absence of pork in that pre-biblical diet; the ancestors of the Jews had eaten a kosher diet before they became Jews. The difference is evidential-contextual. There was no reason for pork-eating Israelites to "hide" their bones over hundreds of years. But subjects of totalitarian regimes had every reason not to generate evidence for their opposition to the regime.

Ignoring evidence for the context of evidence also may lead historians to take evidence at face value rather than decode the information signals and trace them to their sources. For example, neo-totalitarian historians uncritically use totalitarian propaganda as evidence. The Nazis attempted to present anti-Semitism as spontaneous and popular. Stalinist show trials, rather than secret executions, were designed to justify, scapegoat, and implicate. "Spontaneous" telegrams from factory councils demanded "death to the traitors." Both regimes required participation in state rituals, voting, demonstrations, and the signing of "petitions." Uncritical historians and propagandists use this manufactured propaganda for the purposes it was intended. They neglect to use contextual evidence for coercion, terror, and disinformation to decode the nonliteral signal in the noise.

Underdetermining evidence may be consistent with a range of underdetermined historiographic inferences, while sufficing for falsifying other historiographic hypotheses outside that range. For example, evidence is limited for the popularity of the Nazi and Communist regimes at various periods in the absence of free elections and polling. Though some extreme hypotheses are highly improbable, there is a range of possibilities consistent with the limited evidence. For example, in the elections in 1946, the Czechoslovak Communist Party received 38 percent of the votes; at the exit point from Communism, in the 1990 elections, the Czechoslovak Communist Party received 13 percent of the votes. The exact Communist popularity between the 1948 Revolution and 1990 is a matter of conjecture though it is unlikely to have had a substantial majority at any point, and certainly not following the 1968 Soviet invasion. But historians who wish to defend the legitimacy of totalitarianism exaggerate the probabilities of underdetermined possibilities, to claim vaguely that Nazism or Communism were popular and "anchored in society" (Schulze-Wessel in Mathews 2019) and hence enjoyed democratic legitimacy, without ever winning a majority of the votes in free and fair elections before or after the dictatorship.

Before wrapping up this section about fallacious historiographic reasoning, I want to highlight two conceptual mistakes that some historians make that are not unique to historiography but are present also in social and political theory, and undermine the possibility of language to refer or say anything about history, let alone use historiographic reasoning: *Conceptual deflation by over-inflation* and *conceptual deflation by idealization*. When historians over-inflate the meanings of concepts beyond their ordinary language or technical meanings, they become meaningless. Historiography that uses inflated concepts becomes vacuous. This happens especially when historians use emotionally charged concepts that express righteous anger like "Nazi," "genocide," "colonialism," "apartheid," "anarchists," "Stalinists," "Communists," and for anti-liberal historians even "liberalism" in much broader senses than their ordinary language or technical meanings allow to broaden the moral condemnation of historical atrocities that occurred in particular times and periods to a much broader class of events that they dislike. For example, it is possible to call any case of mass violence in history "genocide," and every historical movement of people, commodities, and ideas "colonialism." But then concepts like genocide and colonialism become vacuous, indistinct from all the other things that happened in history and cannot describe or explain specific events and processes as distinct. Even opposite concepts can be subsumed dialectically under the same inflated conceptual umbrella, for example, "new public management," a euphemism for central planning, is subsumed and condemned under the opposite concept of "Neo-Liberalism," even though if there is one thing liberalism is not, it is central planning. Totalitarianism likewise is subsumed under a concept of popular democracy together with its opposite, "social contract," to claim that the dictatorship had a social contract with its subjects (Schulze-Wessel in Matthews 2019). Such a social contract would have to resemble the "social contract" an armed robber has with a bank. Liberal democracy's tolerance of plurality can be presented as a form of oppression or at least "micro-aggression," indistinguishable from totalitarianism, and so on and on. If concepts are inflated enough to dialectically include their opposites, they become as meaningless as the historiography that uses them.

The opposite conceptual mistake is the over-idealization of concepts that leads to their historical deflation; they do not refer to anything that happened in history. For example, if democracy is over-idealized to demand total political egalitarianism, as the Jacobins interpreted it, there has never been and probably never will be a democracy, though Robespierre chopped and sliced his way in that direction (Talmon 1970). If totalitarianism means the total control of the state of everybody, everywhere, with total loss of any personal autonomy, there has never been totalitarianism on a state level, though some concentration camps and gulags got damned close. If historians abandon the use of such concepts because they have never been realized in history, historiography cannot use concepts to explain the evidence and history. An impoverished historiography that cannot use such colligated concepts (cf. Kuukkanen 2015) can only attempt to infer properties of single events without conceptual tools for comparing them and attempting to answer questions about reasons for historical similarities or differences. Judgments about history founded on such a nonconceptual and non-colligated historiography cannot be comparative but absolute, from an explicit or implicit universal "view from nowhere" perspective that judges each case by itself, or as the case may be, condemn all history as one damned thing after another.

Historians who use fallacious forms of reasoning sometimes attempt to justify their invalid reasoning by baseless philosophy of the history of historiography, by inventing an unfounded teleology of the history of historiography, where passion-driven irrational historiography is the end of the history of historiography, so historiographic reasoning is condemned (as genetics was condemned in the Soviet Union) as "reactionary," and disobedient to "history," to the teleological process the historian has just invented to justify the violation of the rules of historiographic reasoning. Historiographic teleologies, like the much grander theological and political eschatological teleologies that benighted modern history, attempt to appeal to opportunists to become fellow travelers to join the "progressive" cause of ignoring the evidence with a promise of inevitable victorious destiny, while condemning reasoning without having to actually come to terms with it and find some arguments against it, which would have forced the irrationals to play on the rational argumentative field. Of course, anybody can construct equally arbitrary alternative teleologies for historiography as well as for history. Even if history has a *telos*, it does not imply that this end is knowable, especially since history has demonstrated that it has a taste for surprise endings. What if history ends neither with the Kingdom of God, nor with eternal peace, nor with classless society, nor with the victory of liberty, but with a mad orange clown with a red tie?

15 Conclusion: The Historical Sciences

Reasoning in the historical sciences infers properties of historical origins of information signals that are decoded from the evidence. Knowledge of human history "depend[s] on the development of systems to record events and hence accumulate and transmit information about the past. No records, no history, so history is actually synonymous with the information age" (Floridi 2010, 3). Human history before the invention of writing is inferred from other types of information signals such as artefacts, languages, and DNA.

Historiographic reasoning is about tokens. The evidential inputs of historiographic reasoning are tokens, and the inferred historical origins of the evidence are tokens. Evidence and epistemic outputs in the theoretical sciences are types (Sober 1988; Cleland, 2001, 2002, 2009; Tucker 2004, 2012; Turner 2007) For example, theoretical biology is interested in DNA as a theoretical type, whereas historical phylogeny is interested in token historical individual genomes. Theoretical physics is interested in types of particles and theories that model their behavior. Cosmology of the early universe is interested in how tokens of these particles behaved and interacted in the extreme conditions following the Big Bang. Generative linguistics is interested in language as a type. Historical philology is interested in token languages that were spoken by people in particular areas and periods. The distinction between *originary* and *causal* sciences that infer primarily, respectively, the origins of information-preserving evidence and causal relations between theoretical entities absorbs the distinctions between historical and theoretical sciences, and replaces distinctions between sciences according to their domains, for example human versus natural, that became obsolete as soon as psychology established itself as a science of the human mind, or their goals, for example ideographic description versus nomothetic discovery of laws (see Tucker 2012). The distinction between the historical sciences that infer token origins and sciences that infer types of causes cuts through established academic disciplinary boundaries to base the classification of the sciences on firm epistemic foundations and actual distinct scientific methods and practices.

The extent to which historians can and do offer causal explanations of events, or for that matter rational explanations of action or understanding of historical minds, depends entirely on whether information from the past reached receivers in the present that can be decoded to infer origins such as causal chains, rational actions and decisions, or the states of mind of past agents. Models of historiographic explanation, causation, understanding, rational choice, and so on are derived from reasoning about the evidence and depend on the information that reaches the present without equivocation and can be separated from noise, and the availability of theories to decode the information.

Historiographic reasoning is distinct from reasoning in causal sciences such as the social sciences. Yet, this form of reasoning is not unique to the generation of knowledge of human history, but is common to all the historical sciences that generate knowledge of originary sources of information in the past from independent information signals that reached the present and can be decoded: Philologists generated knowledge of originary proto-languages from coherences between languages; Geologists have generated knowledge of the past from distant rock formation that preserved information about their common origins; Evolutionary biologists generated knowledge of origins of species from coherences between homologies of living species and fossils, and more recently from coherences of sequenced genomes; Cosmologists have generated knowledge of the early universe from background radiation. Historiographic reasoning, *mutandis mutatis*, permeates sciences that generate knowledge of the past irrespective of their subject matters and the kinds of information channels they infer to trace the information signals from origins to evidence. This is quite an impressive outcome for the historiographic type of reasoning that was developed originally by pedantic academic philologists in marginal departments in provincial universities in the second half of the eighteenth century.

References

Anava, Sarit, Neuhof, Moran, Gingold, Hila, et al. (2020) "Illuminating Genetic Mysteries of the Dead Sea Scrolls," *Cell*, 181(6), 1218–1231.

Ankersmit, Frank (1995) "Statements, Texts and Pictures," in Frank Ankersmit & Hans Kellner, eds. *A New Philosophy of History*. London: Reaktion Books, 212–240.

Ankersmit, Frank (2001) *Historical Representation*. Palo Alto, CA: Stanford University Press.

Ankersmit, Frank (2012) *Meaning, Truth, and Reference in Historical Representation*. Ithaca, NY: Cornell University Press.

Batty, David (2020) "Court Fines Historian over Claims of Holocaust Survivor's Lesbian Affair," *The Guardian*, December 21.

Ben-Menahem, Yemima (1997) "Historical Contingency," *Ratio*, 10(2), 99–107.

Ben-Menahem, Yemima (2009) "Historical Necessity and Contingency," in Aviezer Tucker, ed., *A Companion to the Philosophy of History and Historiography*. Malden, MA: Wiley-Blackwell, 120–130.

Ben-Menahem, Yemima (2016) "If Counterfactuals Were Excluded from Historical Reasoning …," *Journal of the Philosophy of History*, 10(3), 370–381.

Bertsch-McGrayne, Sharon (2011) *The Theory that Would Not Die: How Bayes' Rule Cracked the Enigma Code, Hunted Down Russian Submarines, & Emerged Triumphant From Two Centuries of Controversy*. New Haven, CT: Yale University Press.

Bloch, Marc (1961). *Feudal Society*. Trans. L. A. Manyon, Chicago, IL: University of Chicago Press.

Bovens, Luc, & Hartmann, Stephan (2003) *Bayesian Epistemology*. Oxford: Oxford University Press.

Buck, Caitlin E., W. G. Cavanagh, & C. D. Litton eds. (1996) *Bayesian Approach to Interpreting Archaeological Data*. Chichester: Wiley.

Burke, Peter (2019) *Eyewitnessing: The Uses of Image as Historical Evidence*. London: Reaktion Books.

Carrier, Richard (2012) *Proving History: Bayes's Theorem and the Quest for the Historical Jesus*. Amherst, NY: Prometheus Books.

Carrier, Richard (2014) *On the Historicity of Jesus: Why We Might Have Reason for Doubt*. Sheffield: Sheffield Phoenix Press.

Cleland, Carol E. (2001) "Historical Science, Experimental Science, and the Scientific Method," *Geology*, 29(11), 987–990.

Cleland, Carol E. (2002) "Methodological and Epistemic Differences between Historical Science and Experimental Science," *Philosophy of Science*, 69, 474–496.

Cleland, Carol E. (2009) "Philosophical Issues in Natural History and Its Historiography," in Avierez Tucker, ed., *A Companion to the Philosophy of History and Historiography*. Malden, MA: Wiley-Blackwell, 44–62.

Cleland, Carol E. (2011) "Prediction and Explanation in Historical Natural Science," *British Journal for the Philosophy of Science*, 62, 551–582.

Coady, David (2004) "Preempting Preemption," in John Collins, Ned Hall, & Laurie A. Paul, eds., *Causation and Counterfactuals*. Cambridge, MA: Massachusetts Institute of Technology Press, 325–340.

Collingwood, Robin G. (1956) *The Idea of History*. Oxford: Oxford University Press.

Collins, Harry M. (2010) *Tacit and Explicit Knowledge*. Chicago, IL: Chicago University Press.

Collins, John (2004) "Preemptive Preemption," in John Collins, Ned Hall, & Laurie A. Paul, eds., *Causation and Counterfactuals*. Cambridge, MA: Massachusetts Institute of Technology Press, 107–117.

Currie, Adrian (2018) *Rock, Bone and Ruin: An Optimist's Guide to the Historical Sciences*. Cambridge, MA: Massachusetts Institute of Technology Press.

D'Amico, Robert (1989) *Historicism and Knowledge*. New York, NY: Routledge.

Danto, Arthur (1985) *Narration and Knowledge (including the integral text of Analytical Philosophy of History)*. New York, NY: Columbia University Press.

Daston, Lorraine (1988) *Classical Probability in the Enlightenment*. Princeton, NJ: Princeton University Press.

De Cecco, Marcello (1985) "Monetary Theory and Roman History," *The Journal of Economic History*, 45, 809–822.

DeRose, Keith (2009) *The Case for Contextualism: Knowledge, Skepticism, and Context, Vol. 1*. Oxford: Oxford University Press.

Dimova-Cookson, Maria (2019) *Rethinking Positive and Negative Liberty*. London: Routledge.

Dummett, Michael (1978) *Truth and Other Enigmas*. Cambridge, MA: Harvard University Press.

Dummett, Michael (2004) *Truth and the Past*. New York, NY: Columbia University Press.

Elster, Jon (1978) *Logic and Society: Contradictions and Possible Worlds*. Chichester: Wiley.

Elster, Jon (1999) *Alchemies of the Mind: Rationality and the Emotions*. New York, NY: Cambridge University Press.

Evans, Richard J. (2016) "Response," *Journal of the Philosophy of History*, 10(3), 457–467.

Felsenstein, Joseph (2004) *Inferring Phylogenies*. Sunderland, MA: Sinauer Associates.

Floridi, Luciano (2010) *Information: A Very Short Introduction*. Oxford: Oxford University Press.

Gadamer, Hans Georg (1989) *Truth and Method*. Trans. Joel Weinsheimer & Donald G. Marshall, London: Sheed & Ward.

Gellner, Ernst (1983) *Nations and Nationalism*. Ithaca, NY: Cornell University Press.

Ginzburg, Carlo (1980) *The Cheese and the Worms: The Cosmos of a Sixteenth Century Miller*. Trans. John & Anna Tedeschi, Baltimore, MD: Johns Hopkins University Press.

Goldstein, Leon J. (1976) *Historical Knowing*. Austin, TX: University of Texas Press.

Goldstein, Leon J. (1996) *The What and the Why of History: Philosophical Essays*. Leiden: Brill.

Gooch, George Peabody (1959) *History and Historians in the Nineteenth Century*. Boston, MA: Beacon Press.

Grafton, Anthony (1990) *Forgers and Critics: Creativity and Duplicity in Western Scholarship*. Princeton, NJ: Princeton University Press.

Grafton, Anthony (1997) *The Footnote, A Curious History*. Cambridge, MA: Harvard University Press.

Grafton, Anthony, Most, Glenn W., & Zetzel, James, E. G. (1985) "Introduction," in Wolf, Friedrich A., *Prolegomena to Homer*. Princeton, NJ: Princeton University Press, 3–25.

Greco, John (2020) *The Transmission of Knowledge*. Cambridge, UK: Cambridge University Press.

Greenhill, Simon J., Heggarty, Paul, & Gray, Russell D. (2020) "Bayesian Phylolinguistics," in Richard D. Janda, Brian D. Joseph, & Barbara S. Vance, eds., *The Handbook of Historical Linguistics*. Hoboken, NJ: Wiley, 226–253.

Hall, Ned (2004a) "Causation and the Price of Transitivity," in John Collins, Ned Hall, & Laurie A. Paul, eds., *Causation and Counterfactuals*. Cambridge, MA: Massachusetts Institute of Technology Press, 181–203.

Hall, Ned (2004b) "Two Concepts of Causation," in John Collins, Ned Hall, & Laurie A. Paul, eds., *Causation and Counterfactuals*. Cambridge, MA: Massachusetts Institute of Technology Press, 225–276.

Himmelfarb, Milton (1984) "No Hitler, No Holocaust," *Commentary Magazine*, 77, 3.

Hobson, Michael P. Andrew H. Jaffe, Andrew R. Liddle, Pia Mukherjee, & David Parkinson, eds. (2010) *Bayesian Methods in Cosmology*. Cambridge, UK: Cambridge University Press.

Inkpen, Rib, & Turner, Derek (2012) "The Topography of Historical Contingency," *Journal of the Philosophy of History*, 6(1), 1–19.

Irwin, Daniel, & Mandel, David R. (2019) "Improving Information Evaluation for Intelligence Production," *Intelligence and National Security*, 34(4), 503–525.

Jardine, Nick (2008) "Explanatory Genealogies and Historical Testimony," *Episteme*, 5, 160–179.

Jensen, Anthony K. (2013) *Nietzsche's Philosophy of History*. Cambridge, UK: Cambridge University Press.

Kosso, Peter (2001) *Knowing the Past: Philosophical Issues of History and Archaeology*. Amherst, NY: Humanity Books.

Kuhn, Thomas (1996) *The Structure of Scientific Revolutions*. Chicago, IL: University of Chicago Press.

Kuukkanen, Jouni-Matti (2015) *Postnarrativist Philosophy of Historiography*. New York, NY: Palgrave.

Laplace, Pierre-Simon (1840) *Essai philosophique sur les probabilités*, 6th Edition, Paris: Bachelier.

Lewis, David (1973) *Counterfactuals*, Oxford: Blackwell.

Lewis, David (1979) "Counterfactual Dependence and Time's Arrow," *Noûs*, 13(4), 455–476.

Lewis, David (1986) *Philosophical Papers* Vol. II. New York, NY: Oxford University Press.

Lewis, David (2004) "Causation as Influence," in John Collins, Ned Hall, & Laurie A. Paul, 2004. *Causation and Counterfactuals*, Cambridge, MA: Massachusetts Institute of Technology Press, 75–106.

Lincoln, Bruce (1999) *Theorizing Myth: Narrative, Ideology, and Scholarship*. Chicago, IL: University of Chicago Press.

Maar, Alexander (2016) "Applying D. K. Lewis's Counterfactual Theory of Causation to the Philosophy of Historiography," *Journal of the Philosophy of History*, 10, 349–369.

Malaterre, Christophe (2024) "Overdetermination, underdetermination, and epistemic granularity in the historical sciences," *European Journal of Philosophy of Science*, 14, 23.

Mandelbaum, Maurice (1977) *The Anatomy of Historical Knowledge*. Baltimore, MD: Johns Hopkins University Press.

Matthews, David (2019) "Czech Totalitarianism Institute Faces Questions over Research," *Times Higher Education*, August 20.

Meinecke, Friedrich (1972) *Historism: The Rise of a New Historical Outlook*. Trans. J. E. Anderson. New York, NY: Herder & Herder.

Momigliano, Arnaldo (1977) *Essays in Ancient and Modern Historiography*, Middletown, CT: Wesleyan University Press.

Morgan, John (2021) "Research Misconduct Ruling on Historian's Holocaust Affair Claim," *Times Higher Education*, February 4, 2021, Online edition.

Murphey, Murray G. (1973) *Our Knowledge of the Historical Past*. Indianapolis, IN: Bobbs-Merrill.

Murphey, Murray G. (1994) *Philosophical Foundations of Historical Knowledge*. Albany, NY: State University of New York Press.

Murphey, Murray G. (2009) *Truth and History*. Albany, NY: State University of New York Press.

Nolan, Daniel (2016) "The Possibilities of History," *Journal of the Philosophy of History*, 10(3), 441–456.

Parry, Milman & Parry, Adam, ed. (1971) *The Making of Homeric Verse: The Collected Papers of Milman Parry*. Oxford: Oxford University Press.

Razi, Zvi (1980) *Life, Marriage, and Death in a Medieval Parish: Economy, Society, and Demography in Halesowen, 1270–1400*. Cambridge: Cambridge University Press.

Ressa, Maria (2023) *How to Stand Up to a Dictator: The Fight for Our Future*. New York, NY: Harper Perennial.

Rood, Tim (2006) "Objectivity and Authority: Thucydides' Historical Method," in *Brill's Companion to Thucydides*, Antoninos Rengakos & Antonis Tsakmakis, eds., Leiden: Brill, 225–249.

Rosenfeld, Gavriel D. (2016) "The Ways We Wonder "What If?": Towards a Typology of Historical Counterfactuals," *Journal of the Philosophy of History*, *10*(3), 382–411.

Roth, Paul A. (2012) "The Pasts," *History and Theory*, 51, 313–339.

Sabar, Ariel (2020) *Veritas: A Harvard Professor, a Con Man and the Gospel of Jesus's Wife*. New York, NY: Anchor.

Salmon, Wesley C. (1998) "Rationality and Objectivity in Science or Tom Kuhn Meets Tom Bayes," in Martin Curd & J. A. Cover, eds., *Philosophy of Science: The Central Issues*, New York, NY: W. W. Norton, 551–583.

Santayana, George (1954) *The Life of Reason, or The Phases of Human Progress*. New York, NY: Scribner.

Schaffer, Jonathan (2004) "Trumping Preemption," in John Collins, Ned Hall, & Laurie A. Paul, eds., *Causation and Counterfactuals*. Cambridge, MA: Massachusetts Institute of Technology Press, 59–73.

Serrier, Thomas & Stéphane Michonneau (2019) "One heritage, one story: That's not the Europe we know," *The Guardian*, 17 April 2019.

Shannon, Claude Elwood (1964) *The Mathematical Theory of Communication*. Urbana IL: University of Illinois Press.

Snyder, Timothy (2015) *Black Earth: The Holocaust as History and Warning*. New York, NY: Tim Duggan Books.

Sunstein, Cass R. (2016) "Historical Explanations Always Involve Counterfactual History," *Journal of the Philosophy of History*, 10(3), 433–440.

Sober, Elliott (1988) *Reconstructing the Past: Parsimony, Evolution, and Inference*. Cambridge, MA: Massachusetts Institute of Technology Press.

Sterelny, Kim (2016) "Contingency and History." *Philosophy of Science*, 8(4), 521–539.

Talmon, J. L. (1970) *The Origins of Totalitarian Democracy*. New York, NY: Norton.

Taylor, Arthur John, ed., (1975) *The Standard of Living in Britain in the Industrial Revolution*. London: Methuen.

Tucker, Aviezer (2004) *Our Knowledge of the Past: A Philosophy of Historiography*. Cambridge, UK: Cambridge University Press.

Tucker, Aviezer (2006) "Temporal Provincialism: Anachronism, Retrospection and Evidence," *Scientia Poetica*, 10, 299–317.

Tucker, Aviezer (2009) "The Philosophy of Natural History and Historiography," review of: Derek Turner, *Making Prehistory: Historical Science and the Scientific Realism Debate* (Cambridge: Cambridge University Press, 2007) and Rob Inkpen, *Science, Philosophy and Physical Geography* (London: Routledge, 2005), *Journal of the Philosophy of History*, 3, 385–394.

Tucker, Aviezer (2012) "Sciences of Tokens and Types: The Difference between History and the Social Sciences," in Harold Kincaid, ed., *The Oxford Handbook of Philosophy of the Social Sciences*, Oxford: Oxford University Press, 274–297.

Tucker, Aviezer (2014) "Epistemology as a Social Science: Applying the Neuman-Rubin Method to Explain Expert Beliefs," in Carlo Martini & Marcel Boumans, eds., *Experts and Consensus in Social Science*, Dordrecht: Springer, 155–170.

Tucker, Aviezer (2016) "The Malthusian Holocaust: Review of Timothy Snyder, *Black Earth: The Holocaust as History and Warning*," *The American Interest*, 11(5), (2016), 76–88.

Tucker, Aviezer (2020) "Origins and Genealogies," in Anthony Jensen & Carlotte Santini, eds., *Nietzsche on Memory and History: the Re-Encountered Shadow*, Berlin: de Gruyter, 57–75.

Tucker, Aviezer (2021) "Forbidding Fruit: Apple TV+ Does Asimov: Asimov's *Foundation* stories are a thought experiment in the social sciences," *American Purpose*, October 8, online.

Tucker, Aviezer (2023) "Critical Reliability: A Bayesian Program for Intelligence Analysis," *Journal of Intelligence & Analysis*, 26(1), 76–96.

Tucker, Aviezer (2024) "Historiographic Populist Emotivism," in Berber Bevernage, Eline Mestdagh, Walderez Ramalho & Marie-Gabrielle Verbergt, eds., *Claiming the People's Past: Populist Politics of History in the Twenty-First Century*. Cambridge, UK: Cambridge University Press, 248–266.

Tucker, Aviezer & Adam Garfinkle (2018) "The Etiology of Faked News," *The American Interest*, 14(1), 31–35.

Turner, Derek (2007) *Making Prehistory: Historical Science and the Scientific Realism Debate*. Cambridge, UK: Cambridge University Press.

Van Dam, Andrew (2024) "Why Are Republicans More Likely to Suffer Hearing Loss?" *The Washington Post*, February 9.

Van Fraassen, Bass (1980) *The Scientific Image*. Oxford: Oxford University Press.

Vico, Giambattista (1984) [1744] *The New Science*, trans. Thomas Goddard Bergin & Max Harold Fisch, London, UK: Cornell University Press.

Wallach, Efraim (2018) "Bayesian Representation of a Prolonged Archaeological Debate," *Synthese* 195, 401–431.

White, Hayden (1978) *Tropics of Discourse*. Baltimore, MD: Johns Hopkins University Press.

White, Hayden (1987) *The Content of the Form*. Baltimore, MD: Johns Hopkins University Press.

White, Hayden (1992) "Historical Emplotment and the Problem of Truth," in Saul Friedlander, ed., *Probing the Limits of Representation: Nazism and the "Final Solution,"* Cambridge, MA: Harvard University Press, 37–53.

Windelband, Wilhelm (2015) "Critical or Genetic Method (1883)," in Sebastian Luft, ed., *The Neo-Kantian Reader*, New York, NY: Routledge, 271–286.

Wolf, Friedrich A. (1985) *Prolegomena to Homer*, Trans. Anthony Grafton, Glenn W. Most, & James E. G. Zetzel, Princeton, NJ: Princeton University Press, 3–25.

Wolin, Richard (2013) "Biblical Blame Shift: Is the Egyptologist Jan Assmann Fueling Anti-Semitism?" *The Chronicle of Higher Education*, April 15.

Woolf, Daniel (2016) "Concerning Altered Pasts: Reflections of an Early Modern Historian," *Journal of the Philosophy of History*, 10(3), 413–432.

Acknowledgments

This Element is based on a creative integration and synthesizing rework of articles I published in the twenty years since I published *Our Knowledge of the Past: A Philosophy of Historiography* (Tucker 2004). The adage that "the whole is greater than the sum of its parts" is particularly appropriate to describe this result.

I have expanded the theoretical framework I developed in my 2004 book to encompass a broader scope of topics. Yet, I still own most of the arguments in *Our Knowledge of the Past*. The one major change in my thinking since that book is ontological and by implication epistemic: In *Our Knowledge of the Past* I considered historiographic inference of knowledge of history a type of inference of *common cause*. I conceived history, the past, as causing the present, and historiography, representations of history, as inferring common causes, historical events and processes, from their contemporary effects. I was critical of philosophical discussions of the inference of common cause that emerged from the philosophy of physics, and did not consider how historical sciences inferred common causes. Elliott Sober and Carol Cleland developed similar arguments, though I disputed some of the details and concentrated on historiographic knowledge of human history, whereas they were more concerned, respectively, with the history of life and phylogeny and natural history. Gradually, though, I came to the conclusion that the inference of common cause is too general for understanding historiographic reasoning. Concurrently, I realized that the fundamental ontology of historiography and the historical sciences is not of causes and effect, but of origins, information transmission signals and channels, and information-preserving evidence in the present. Together, the new ontology and epistemology imply that rather than infer or retrodict past common causes from their effects, the historical sciences infer common origins, information sources, from receivers of information signals that preserve information from the past and are connected to their origins through information channels. This ontological change led to a more parsimonious and accurate reformulation of the epistemology of historiography and the historical sciences that explains better historiographic practices. I articulated best these issues and my reasons for the ontological shift in what I consider my most important single article in the philosophy of historiography since I published *Our Knowledge of the Past*: "The Inferences of Common Causes Reduced to Common Origins," *Studies in History and Philosophy of Science Part A*, volume 81, June 2020, 105–115.

This Element is not a collection of previously published articles, but their synthesis, a creative integration into a cohesive whole that is greater than the sum of its parts. I should acknowledge the origins of this synthetic integration in the following published articles and reviews, listed chronologically: "Temporal Provincialism: Anachronism, Retrospection and Evidence," *Scientia Poetica*, Vol. 10 (2006), 299–317; "Historiographic Revision and Revisionism: The Evidential Difference," in Michal Kopecek, ed., *Past in the Making: Recent History and Historical Revisionism* (Budapest: Central European University Press, 2008), 1–16; "Historical Science, Over- and Under-determined: A Study of Darwin's Inference of Origins," *The British Journal for the Philosophy of Science*, Vol. 62, 2011, 825–849; "Sciences of Tokens and Types: The Difference between History and the Social Sciences," in Harold Kincaid, ed., *The Oxford Handbook of Philosophy of the Social Sciences* (Oxford: Oxford University Press, 2012), 274–297; "Historical Truth," in Vittorio Hosle, ed., *Forms of Truth and the Unity of Knowledge*, (South Bend, IN: Notre Dame University Press, 2014), 232–259; "Epistemology as a Social Science: Applying the Neuman–Rubin Method to Explain Expert Beliefs," in Carlo Martini & Marcel Boumans eds., *Experts and Consensus in Social Science*, (Dordrecht: Springer, 2014), 155–170; "Historiographic Ancients and Moderns: The Difference between Thucydides and Ranke," in Alexandra Lianeri, ed., *Knowing Future Time in and through Greek Historiography, Trends in Classics – Supplementary Volume,* 32, (Berlin: de Gruyter, 2016), 361–384; "The Malthusian Holocaust: Review of Timothy Snyder, *Black Earth: The Holocaust as History and Warning*," *The American Interest*, Vol. 11 No. 5, (2016), 76–88. "Historiographic Counterfactuals and the Philosophy of Historiography: An Introduction," *Journal of the Philosophy of History*, Vol. 10 (2016) No. 3, 333–348; Review of: Richard C. Carrier, *Proving History: Bayes's Theorem and the Quest for the Historical Jesus*. Amherst, NY: Prometheus Press, 2012. *History and Theory*, 55, (2016), 129–140. "The Generation of Probable Facts from Testimonies in Jurisprudence and Historiography," *Storia della Storiografia*, 76/2, 2019, 47–62; "Origins and Genealogies," in Anthony Jensen & Carlotte Santini eds., *Nietzsche on Memory and History: The Re-Encountered Shadow* (Berlin: de Gruyter, 2020), 57–75; "Forbidding Fruit: Apple TV+ Does Asimov: Asimov's *Foundation* Stories are a Thought Experiment in the Social Sciences," *American Purpose*, October 8, 2021 (electronic); "Review of Adrian Currie, *Rock, Bone, and Ruin: An Optimist's Guide to the Historical Sciences*," *Journal of the Philosophy of History*, 15–1 (2021), 125–131; "Historicism Now: Historiographic Ontology, Epistemology and Methodology Out of Bounds," *The Journal of Philosophy of History*, 16 (2022), 92–121; "Critical Reliability: A Bayesian Program for

Intelligence analysis," *Journal of Intelligence & Analysis*, Vol. 26 No. 1 (2023), 76–96; Historiographic Populist Emotivism, in Berber Bevernage, Eline Mestdagh, Walderez Ramalho, & Marie-Gabrielle Verbergt eds., *Claiming the People's Past: Populist Politics of History in the Twenty-First Century,* (Cambridge, UK: Cambridge University Press, 2024), 248–266.

Vico thought history follows courses and recourses, linear change and cyclical repetition. Vico's Ideal Eternal History can be modeled as a coiled spring, repeating itself, but on different levels. In writing this Element I experienced something akin to Vico's course and recourse: Some thirty years ago, when I was teaching at Palacky University in the town of Olomouc in Moravia (the eastern half of the Czech Republic), I authored the entries on philosophy of historiography and history for *A Global Encyclopedia of Historical Writing* (New York: Garland, 1998) whose editor was the historian Daniel Woolf, then at Dalhousie University in Canada. Since 1998 I have worked for many years in the United States, but also in Australia, the United Kingdom, and Germany and published on topics in the philosophy of historiography but also in historiography, political theory and philosophy, intellectual history, and epistemology. But now, I am back in Moravia, having just cofounded an academic Centre for the Philosophy of Historiography at The University of Ostrava, and again, I write on the philosophy of historiography for a series edited by the same Daniel Woolf. As Yogi Berra paraphrased Vico, its "déjà vu all over again!" Repeating life on a higher level!

This book has been produced with the financial support of the European Union under the REFRESH – Research Excellence For REgion Sustainability and High-tech Industries project number CZ.10.03.01/00/22_003/0000048 via the Operational Programme Just Transition by the Faculty of Arts at the University of Ostrava.

Cambridge Elements ☰

Historical Theory and Practice

Daniel Woolf
Queen's University, Ontario

Daniel Woolf is Professor of History at Queen's University, where he served for ten years as Principal and Vice-Chancellor, and has held academic appointments at a number of Canadian universities. He is the author or editor of several books and articles on the history of historical thought and writing, and on early modern British intellectual history, including most recently *A Concise History of History* (CUP 2019). He is a Fellow of the Royal Historical Society, the Royal Society of Canada, and the Society of Antiquaries of London. He is married with 3 adult children.

Editorial Board

About the Series
Cambridge Elements in Historical Theory and Practice is a series intended for a wide range of students, scholars, and others whose interests involve engagement with the past. Topics include the theoretical, ethical, and philosophical issues involved in doing history, the interconnections between history and other disciplines and questions of method, and the application of historical knowledge to contemporary global and social issues such as climate change, reconciliation and justice, heritage, and identity politics.

Cambridge Elements ≡

Historical Theory and Practice

Printed in the United States
by Baker & Taylor Publisher Services